BATTLEFIELD WEAPONS AND UNIFORMS OF WORLD WAR II

BATTLEFIELD WEAPONS AND UNIFORMS OF WORLD WAR II

PROJECT COORDINATOR
FRANS SMITS, JR.,
Deputy Curator
Department of Dutch Military
History and Uniforms

CHARTWELL BOOKS INC.

PROJECT COORDINATOR
FRANS SMITS, JR., Deputy Curator
Department of Dutch Military History and Uniforms

COLOR PHOTOGRAPHY
LINDA McCABE

BLACK AND WHITE PHOTOGRAPHY
W.P.M. VAN DER MARK

BOOK DESIGN
JACQUES CHAZAUD

INTRODUCTION
W. HELDER, Director
Royal Dutch Arms and Army Museum "Generaal Hoefer"
Leiden–Delft, The Netherlands

Published by Chartwell Books Inc.,
A Division of Book Sales Inc.,
110 Enterprise Avenue,
Secaucus, New Jersey 07094

© 1978 Peebles Press International, Inc.
ISBN 0-85690-063-x
Library of Congress Catalogue Card Number 77-20714

Printed and bound in the United States of America

CONTENTS

The collections of the Royal Dutch Arms and Army Museum "Generaal Hoefer" contain a great number of life sized mannequins of soldiers of the past. Some sixty of these soldiers are represented in this book.

What is the reason for their existence and their presence in our museum collection?

After the second world war when our Museum awoke from its inevitable enforced slumber during the German occupation of the Netherlands, it had to face the task of modernizing its display. Fortunately it was able to employ some fine artists and craftsmen for this purpose.

The museum is the official Dutch army museum so its first duty is the display of the history of the Dutch ground forces. However, the museum management has the liberty of paying ample attention to the role of the forces of the allies and enemies of the Netherlands in past armed conflicts. This led to the making of dummies of soldiers of the recent military history, which finally resulted in a collection of some 300 soldiers of many countries from all over the world.

We at the museum are particularly proud, not only of the breadth as well as detail of our exhibits, but the extraordinary life-like quality of the mannequins. I hope you will agree that their faces display national characteristics that seem to impart to them a feeling of ongoing activity and spirit that blends magically with the uniforms that they wear.

In many ways this book is a living testament to all soldiers of the sixteen nations represented and we are delighted to participate in the presentation of this very vital period in our recent history.

From every point of view, this book provides an unusually clear picture of the look and feel of the battlefields of World War II.

W. Helder, Director
Royal Dutch Arms and Army
Museum "Generaal Hoefer"
Leiden-Delft, The Netherlands

THE
UNIFORMS

JAPAN
Light Machine Gunner 1st Class
Japanese Infantry

AUSTRALIA
Corporal
Australian Infantry

BELGIUM
Private
Belgian Infantry

GERMANY
Private
German Infantry

CHINA
Corporal
Chinese Troops
Under General Stilwell

CHINA
Soldier
Red Chinese Guerilla Troops
of Mao Tse-tung

DUTCH EAST INDIES
Private 1st Class KNIL
Royal Dutch Indian Army

JAPAN
Corporal
Japanese Infantry

DUTCH EAST INDIES
European Sergeant KNIL
Royal Dutch Indian Army

FINLAND
Private
Finnish Infantry
Winter Uniform

FRANCE
Corporal
3rd Regiment French Foreign Legion

FRANCE

French Resistance Movement

FRANCE
Private
Colonial French Infantry

GERMANY
Sergeant Major (Oberscharführer)
Waffen SS Regiment

GREAT BRITAIN
Private 1st Class
Coldstream Guards
B.E.F. (British Expeditionary Forces)

FRANCE
Warrant Officer
French Tank Battalion No. 503

GERMANY
Lieutenant-Colonel
89th Infantry Regiment

GERMANY
Private 1st Class (Gefreiter)
German Paratroopers

GERMANY
1st Lieutenant
German Antiaircraft Artillery (Flak)

GERMANY
Sergeant (Feldwebel)
'Feldpolizei'

GERMANY
Corporal (Obergefreiter)
German Infantry Regiment

GERMANY
Sergeant Telegraphist (Feldwebel)
German Infantry

GERMANY
Corporal 1st Class
German Coast Artillery

GERMANY

Sergeant (Wachtmeister)

German Antiaircraft Artillery (Flak)

USSR

Soldier

Russian Infantry

Winter Uniform

GERMANY

German Prisoner (SchutzHaftling)
German Concentration Camp

GERMANY

Member of the S.A.
(Sturmabteilung)
of the NSDAP

GREAT BRITAIN
Pilot
R.A.F.

GERMANY
1st Lieutenant
German Luftwaffe

GERMANY
Private
German Infantry
Winter Uniform Eastern Front

USSR
Private
Siberian Contingents
Autumn Uniform

GERMANY
Soldier
Waffen SS Regiment

GERMANY
Soldier with Panzerfaust
German Infantry

GREAT BRITAIN
Major
Parachute Regiment

GREAT BRITAIN
Corporal
The Scots Guards

GREAT BRITAIN
Private 1st Class (Lance-Corporal)
Royal Signal Regiment

GREAT BRITAIN
Corporal
The Queen's Royal Surrey Regiment

GREAT BRITAIN
Women's Health Service
Army Territorial Service

HOLLAND
Private 1st Class
Royal Dutch Brigade "Princess Irene"

HOLLAND

Private
Dutch Depot Battalion

HOLLAND
Officer
Dutch Resistance

HOLLAND
Member of the WA (Weerbaarheidsafdeling)
NSB (Nationalist Socialist Movement)

ITALY
Private
Italian Infantry

ITALY
Soldier
Bersaglieri

ITALY
Soldier of the Student Battalion
Fascist Militia

JAPAN
Officer
Tropical Uniform

JAPAN
Soldier
Japanese Infantry

POLAND
Private
Polish Army

POLAND
Soldier
1st Polish People's Army

RUMANIA
Corporal
8th Rumanian Infantry Regiment

USA
Private 1st Class
7th American Armored Division

USA
Technical Sergeant
3rd US Infantry Division

USA
Paratrooper

USA
Sergeant
2nd US Infantry Division

USA
Marine
USMC

USSR
Sergeant of the Guard
Russian Infantry
Summer Uniform

USSR
Junior Sergeant
Russian Infantry
Winter Uniform

USSR
Private
Russian Guard
Infantry
Autumn Uniform

USSR
Woman Soldier
Military Police Traffic

YUGOSLAVIA
Woman Freedom Fighter (Partisan)
Resistance Army Under Tito

THE EQUIPMENT

AUSTRALIA

Corporal
Australian Infantry
1943-1945

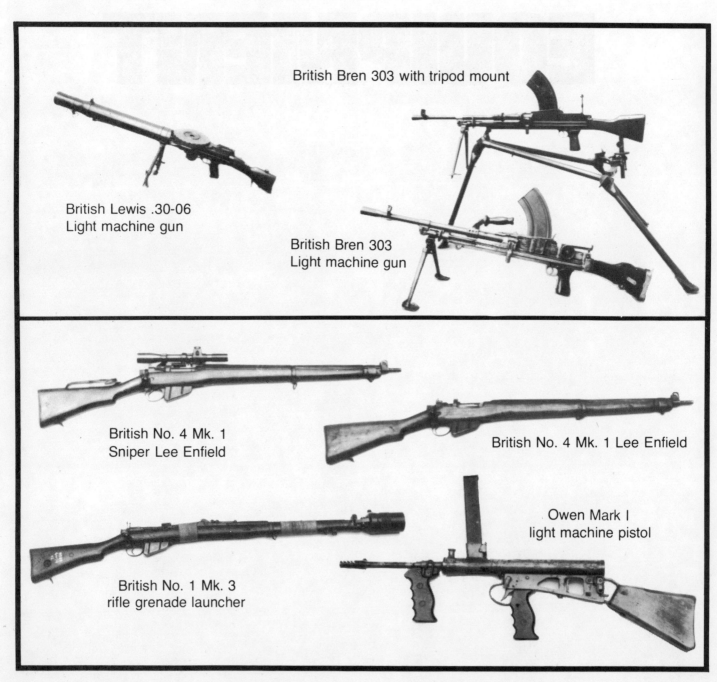

British Bren 303 with tripod mount

British Lewis .30-06
Light machine gun

British Bren 303
Light machine gun

British No. 4 Mk. 1
Sniper Lee Enfield

British No. 4 Mk. 1 Lee Enfield

British No. 1 Mk. 3
rifle grenade launcher

Owen Mark I
light machine pistol

Hat issued to the
New Zealand troops

U.K.
British blue enameled bottle
2nd model webbing   1st model webbing

Gas mask
British Commonwealth issue

Gas mask bag
British Commonwealth issue

British No. 36M
Mills grenade
offensive/defensive

British
smoke hand grenade

British No. 69 Mk. I
offensive hand grenade

British Commonwealth issue
trenching tool in 2 parts

Clip with 5 .303 cartridges
Lee Enfield rifle

BELGIUM

Private
Belgian Infantry
1940, 10th-28th May

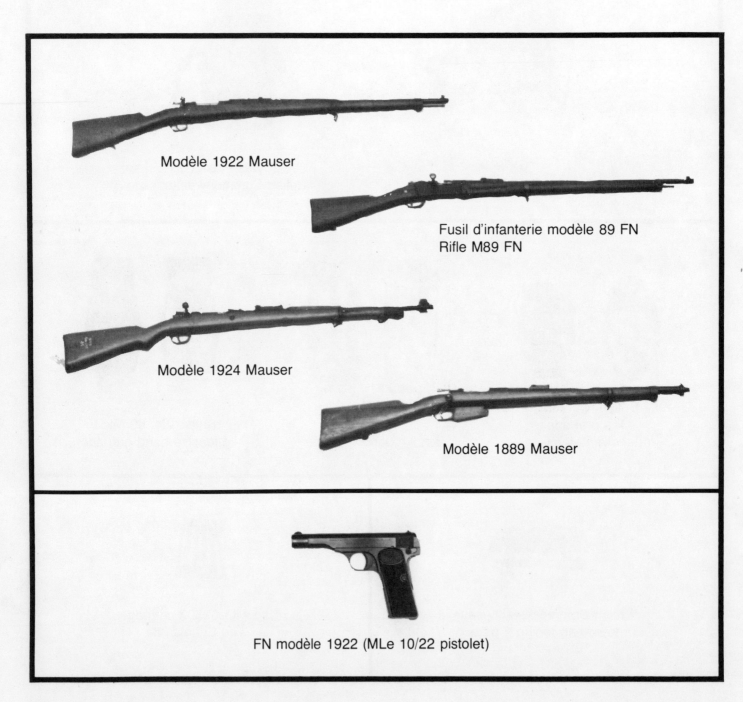

Modèle 1922 Mauser

Fusil d'infanterie modèle 89 FN
Rifle M89 FN

Modèle 1924 Mauser

Modèle 1889 Mauser

FN modèle 1922 (MLe 10/22 pistolet)

Belgian steel helmet M35

Belgian water bottle

Belgian gas mask

Belgian gas mask bag

Belgian defensive
hand grenade

Belgian offensive
hand grenade

Bayonet M 1924

Belgian 7.65 mm. Mauser FN
ammunition

CHINA

Corporal
Chinese troops
under General Stilwell
1942-1945

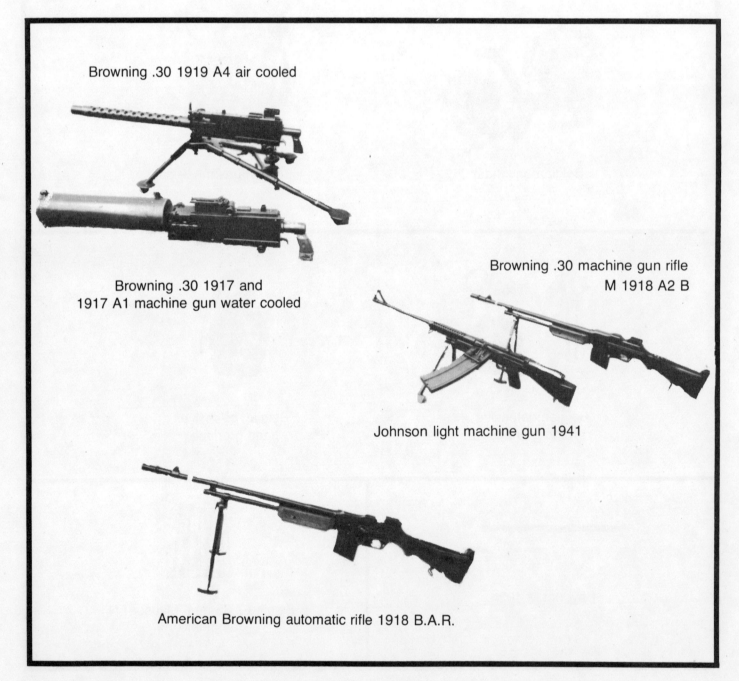

Browning .30 1919 A4 air cooled

Browning .30 1917 and
1917 A1 machine gun water cooled

Browning .30 machine gun rifle
M 1918 A2 B

Johnson light machine gun 1941

American Browning automatic rifle 1918 B.A.R.

American Thompson M1A1
"Tommy" gun

American M3 submachine gun
"grease" gun

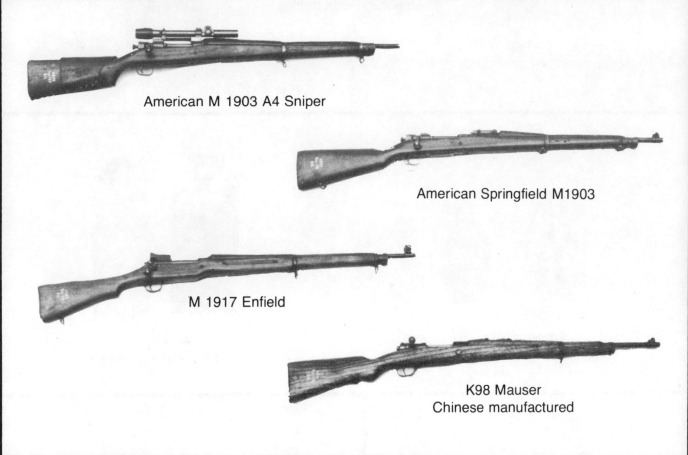

American M 1903 A4 Sniper

American Springfield M1903

M 1917 Enfield

K98 Mauser
Chinese manufactured

American Browning M1911 A1 .45

American
steel helmet M1

American water bottles

American Mk. 2A1
fragmentation defensive grenade

American
smoke hand grenade

American M1 Bayonet

American
.30-06 Springfield
ammunition

German
7.92 mm. Mauser
ammunition

CHINA

Soldier
Red Chinese Guerilla Troops
of Mao Tse-tung
1937-1945

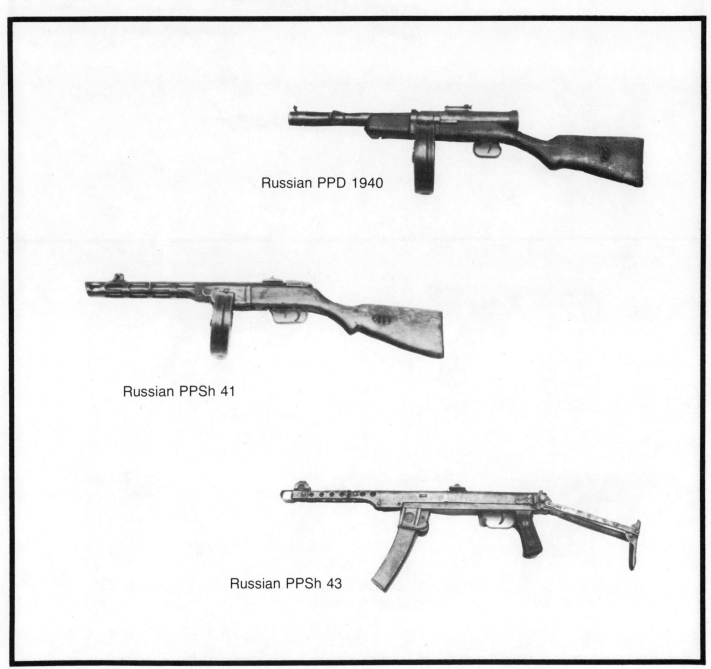

Russian PPD 1940

Russian PPSh 41

Russian PPSh 43

Chinese-built K98 Mauser

Japanese Arisaka
paratrooper
rifle model 2 1942

Japanese Arisaka model 38 (1905)

Japanese Arisaka type 99

Japanese carbine model .38 Arisaka

Japanese model 14 (1925) Nambu

American M 1911 A1 .45

Japanese
type 94 "Shikikenju"

American Smith and Wesson
No. 2 revolver 1917

American Colt
Army .45 M 1917

Fur hat with Communist
Chinese red star emblem

Water bottle (captured Japanese bottle
with KNIL leather frame)

Japanese defensive
hand grenade

Japanese hand grenade
model 91/1931

Japanese
defensive hand grenade

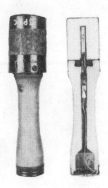

Japanese hand-stick grenade

Russian hand-stick grenade
offensive/defensive
Granata obr R.G.D. 33

Japanese bayonet Arisaka

German/Czechoslovakian
7.92 mm. Mauser
ammunition

Japanese
6.5 mm. Arisaka
ammunition

DUTCH EAST INDIES

European Sergeant KNIL
(Royal Dutch-Indian Army)
1936-1942

Dutch-manufactured M95 (Mannlicher)

Belgian-manufactured
FN pistol M22
(in Holland called M25)

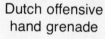

Dutch offensive
hand grenade

Dutch defensive
hand grenade

Dutch steel helmet M34 without emblem
with leather sun-protecting flap

Tropic straw hat
of the KNIL

Dutch East Indian type of water bottle

Trenching tools in 2 parts
for Royal Dutch Indian Army

Dutch gas mask

Dutch bayonet M95 long model

Dutch gas mask bag

Dutch 6.5 mm. M95
ammunition

DUTCH EAST INDIES

Private 1st Class KNIL
armed with "Madsen" machine gun
Royal Dutch Indian Army

Dutch Madsen
6.5 mm. short type

Dutch Madsen 6.5 mm. long type

Dutch-manufactured M95 (Mannlicher)

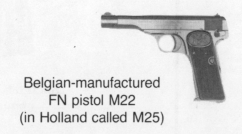

Belgian-manufactured
FN pistol M22
(in Holland called M25)

Dutch steel helmet M34 without emblem
with leather sun-protecting flap

Tropic straw hat
of the KNIL

Dutch East Indies type water bottle

Dutch offensive
hand grenade

Dutch defensive
hand grenade

Dutch gas mask

Dutch gas mask bag

Dutch bayonet M95 long model

Trenching tools in 2 parts
for Royal Dutch East Indian Army

Dutch 6.5 mm. M95
ammunition

FINLAND

Private
Finnish Infantry
Winter Uniform
Karelia and North Finland Campaign
1941-1944

M 1931 Lahti
in Finland known as Suomi

German K98

Lahti 1935
(Swedish version M40)

German 7.92 mm. Mauser
ammunition

Field cap with
Finnish national emblem

German steel helmet M16
used in the Finnish army

FRANCE

Corporal
3rd Regiment French Foreign Legion
Western Front, Germany, Austria
1944-1945

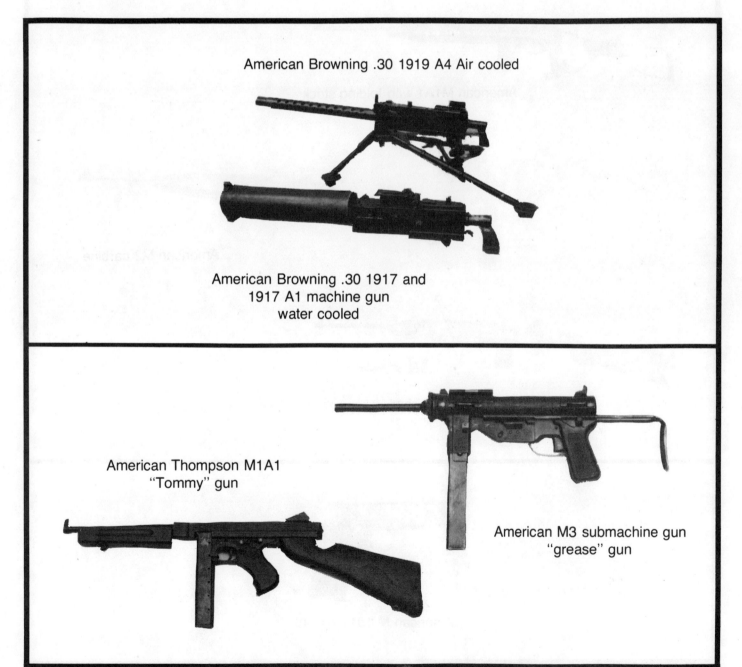

American Browning .30 1919 A4 Air cooled

American Browning .30 1917 and
1917 A1 machine gun
water cooled

American Thompson M1A1
"Tommy" gun

American M3 submachine gun
"grease" gun

American M1 Garand sniper

American Garand M1

American M1A1 with folding stock
paramodel

American M2 carbine

American M1A1 with launcher
rifle grenade

American M 1911 A1 .45

French steel helmet
M 1935

American steel helmet
M1

American water bottle

American water bottle

American Mk. 2A1 fragmentation
defensive grenade

American smoke grenade

American bayonet

American
.30-06 Garand
ammunition

American
.30 carbine M1
ammunition

American trenching tool

FRANCE

Member of the French Resistance
Maquisard des FFI
Hautes-Pyrenées
1943-1944

British Bren .303 light machine gun with tripod mount

British Bren .303 light machine gun

German Kar. 98k

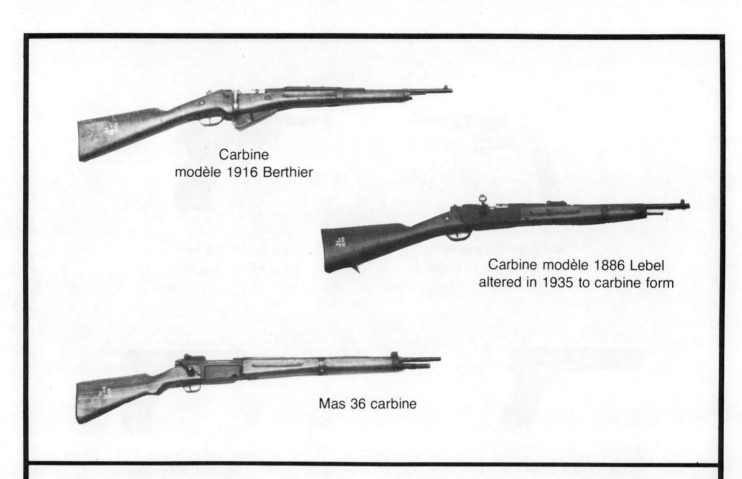

Carbine
modèle 1916 Berthier

Carbine modèle 1886 Lebel
altered in 1935 to carbine form

Mas 36 carbine

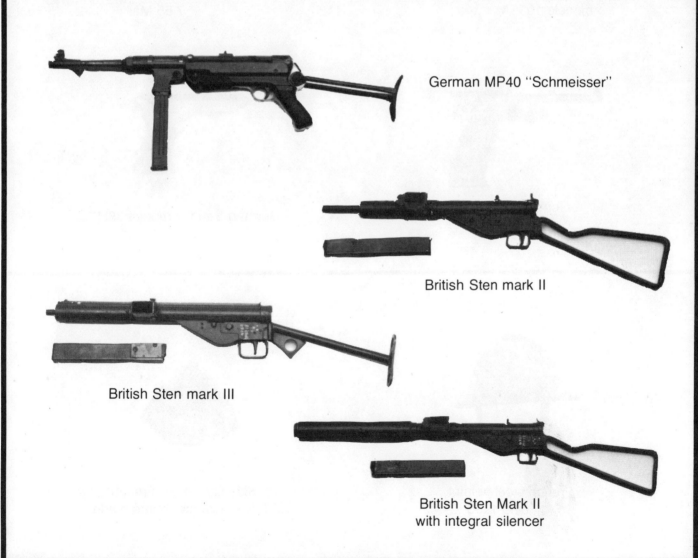

German MP40 "Schmeisser"

British Sten mark II

British Sten mark III

British Sten Mark II
with integral silencer

Revolver modèle 1892
d'ordonnance or Lebel

German M08 9 mm.
parabellum "Luger"

Pistolet automatique
modèle 1935A

Pistolet automatique
7.65 Mas

German pistole 38
(P38) Walther

German Sauer's modell 38H

French steel helmet
modèle 1935

Side cap of the French
F.F.I. resistance (home made)

German offensive hand grenade

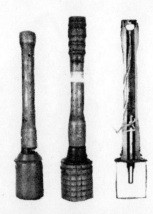

German hand-stick grenade
models 24 and 39 (Stiel handgranaten)

British No. 36M Mills hand grenade
offensive/defensive

French "grenade à main"
offensive O.F.

Bayonet for Fusil Lebel

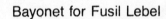

Long model

Short model

French water bottle or bidon

German
7.92 Mauser
ammunition

8 mm. Lebel
ammunition

8 mm. Lebel
ammunition

8 mm. Lebel carbine
ammunition

FRANCE

Private
Colonial French Infantry
May 1940

Heavy machine gun St. Étienne modèle 1907 8 mm.

Light machine gun 7.5 mm.
1924 Chatellerault

Light machine gun M31 Chatellerault

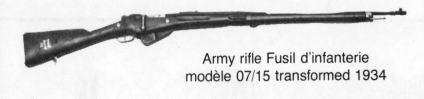

Army rifle Fusil d'infanterie
modèle 07/15 transformed 1934

Army rifle Fusil d'infanterie
modèle 1886/1893 Lebel

French steel helmet M35
(smaller model and
other color for colonial troops)

French side cap

French water bottle or bidon

French gas masks and gas mask bag

French hand grenade
"grenade à main" defensive F.I.

French hand grenade
"grenade à main" offensive O.F.

Long bayonet for Fusil Lebel
(Lebel rifle)

8 mm. Lebel
ammunition

8 mm. Lebel
carbine ammunition

FRANCE

Warrant officer
French Tank Battalion No. 503
1940 Belgian,
Central France Campaign

Carbine
modèle 1916 Berthier

Carbine modèle 1886 Lebel
altered in 1935 to carbine form

Carbine Mas 36

Light machine pistol Mas 38

Revolver modèle 1892
d'ordonnance or Lebel

Automatic pistol
(pistolet automatique modèle 1935A)

Automatic pistol
7.65 Mas

French tank helmet
model 1935

French water bottle or bidon

French gas masks and gas mask bag

French hand grenade
"grenade à main" defensive F.I.

French hand grenade
"grenade à main" offensive O.F.

8 mm. Lebel
ammunition

8 mm. Lebel
carbine ammunition

GERMANY

Private 1st Class (Gefreiter)
German paratroopers
Mediterranean area,
Crete, Greece, Italy
1942-1944

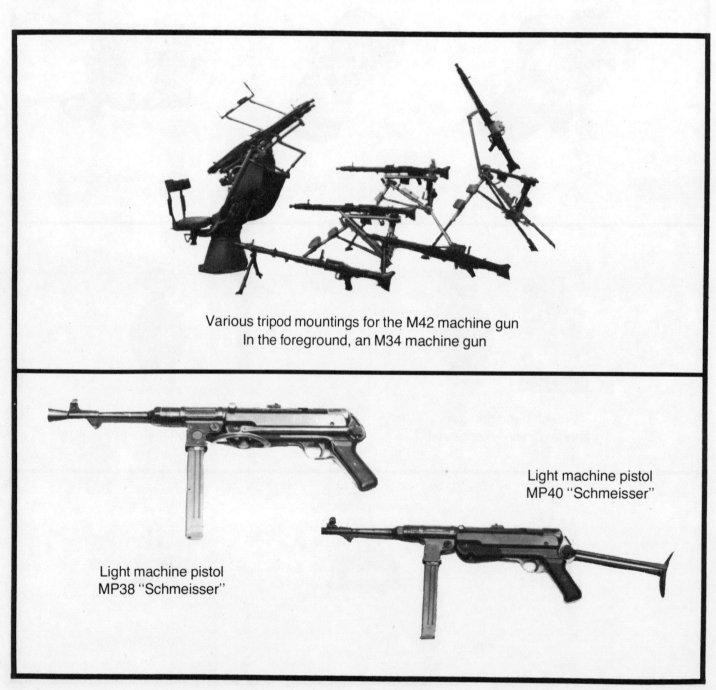

Various tripod mountings for the M42 machine gun
In the foreground, an M34 machine gun

Light machine pistol
MP40 "Schmeisser"

Light machine pistol
MP38 "Schmeisser"

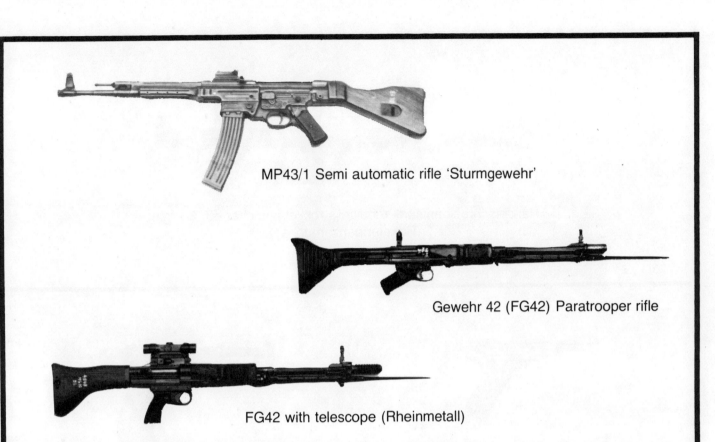

MP43/1 Semi automatic rifle 'Sturmgewehr'

Gewehr 42 (FG42) Paratrooper rifle

FG42 with telescope (Rheinmetall)

Gew. 43 (Kar. 43) Selbstladegewehr

Kar. 98k with rifle grenade launcher

Gewehr 41(m) Selbstladegewehr

Kar. 98k

Kar. 98k with small 1.5 x 2f42 telescope

Panzerschreck antitank recoilless rocket launcher 43, 88 mm.
(Raketenpanzerbuchse)

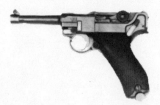

Pistole M08 9 mm. Parabellum "Luger"

Pistole 38 (P38) Walther

German paratrooper helmet with parastrap
with tan colored cover

German gas masks and metal gas mask box

Water bottle,
standard issued to the Army,
Navy, Airforce and Party units.

German water bottle
with bakelite drinking glass
(specially made for tropical use)

German offensive hand grenade

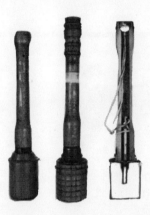

German hand-stick grenades
models 24 and 39 (Stiel handgranaten)

Bayonet
for Mauser K98

German/Czechoslovakian 7.92 mm.
Mauser ammunition

German spade in leather frame

7.92 mm. Mauser
ammunition

7.92 mm. Kurz 43 (short)
ammunition

GERMANY

Lieutenant-Colonel
89th Infantry Regiment
1939-1945

Pistole M08
9 mm. Parabellum "Luger"

Pistole 38 (P38) Walther

Pistole Sauer's modell 38H

Field cap of the Wehrmacht
model 43 (Einheitsmütze)

Steel Helmet M42 Wehrmacht

Officer's cap
of the Wehrmacht

Water bottle
issued to the Army, Navy,
Airforce and Party units

German gas masks and metal gas mask box

GERMANY

1st Lieutenant
German FLAK (Antiaircraft)
Afrika Korps
North Africa Campaign
1942-1943

Pistole M08 9 mm. Parabellum "Luger"

Pistole 38 (P38) Walther

Field cap of the Luftwaffe
sun bleached light Khaki (sand-farbe)

M35 Luftwaffe helmet

Sun helmet of the Afrika Korps
made of cork, olive green cover

German water bottle
special design for the Afrika Korps

German gas mask and metal gas mask box

GERMANY

Private
German Infantry
1939-1942

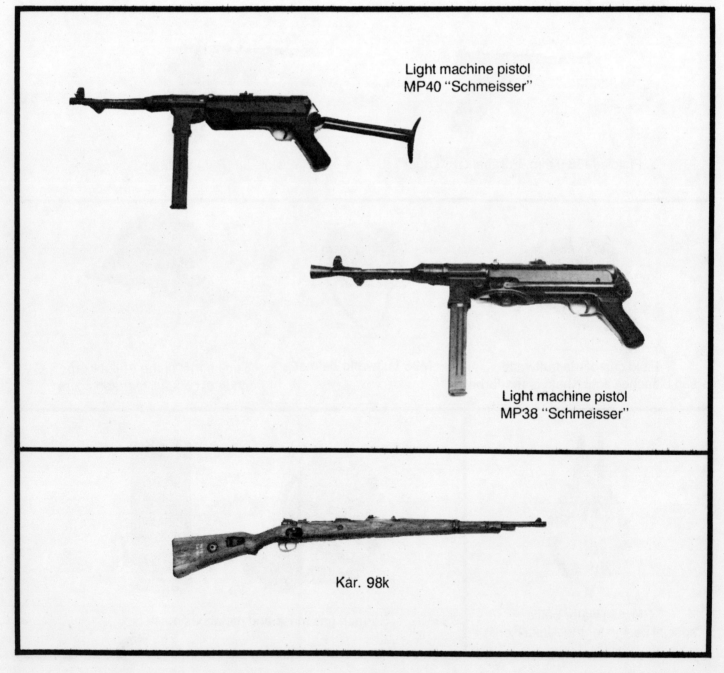

Light machine pistol
MP40 "Schmeisser"

Light machine pistol
MP38 "Schmeisser"

Kar. 98k

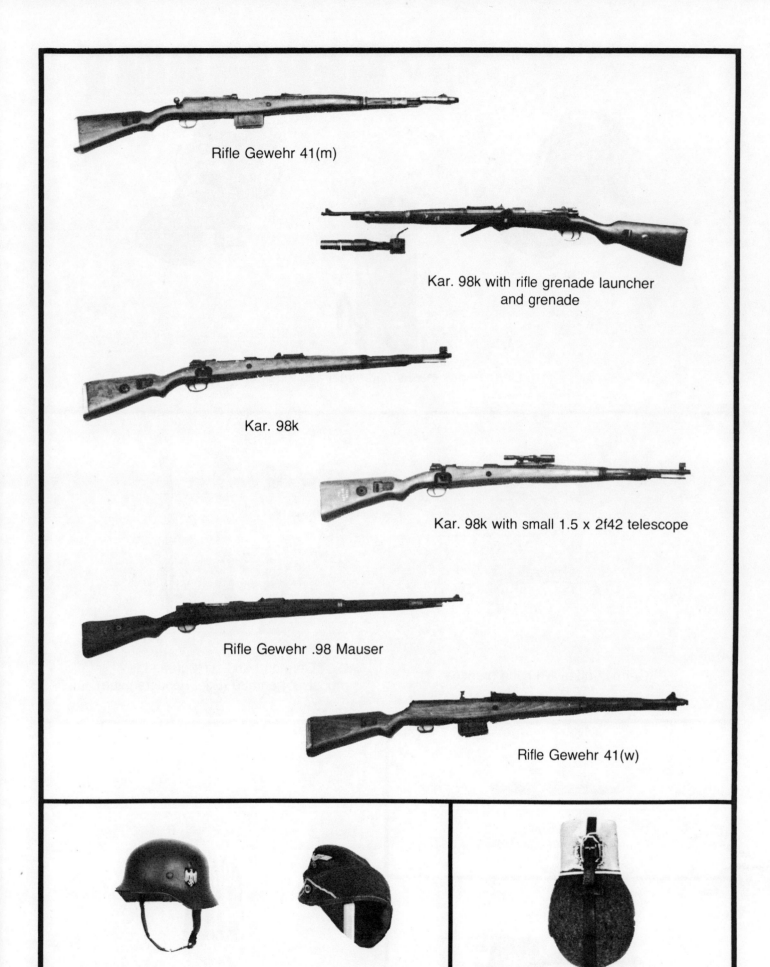

Rifle Gewehr 41(m)

Kar. 98k with rifle grenade launcher
and grenade

Kar. 98k

Kar. 98k with small 1.5 x 2f42 telescope

Rifle Gewehr .98 Mauser

Rifle Gewehr 41(w)

Steel helmet M42

Side cap
of the Wehrmacht

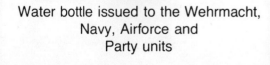

Water bottle issued to the Wehrmacht,
Navy, Airforce and
Party units

German gas masks and metal gas mask box

German offensive hand grenade

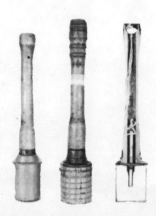

German hand-stick grenades
models 24 and 39 (Stiel handgranaten)

Bayonet
for Mauser Kar. 98k

7.92 mm. Mauser
ammunition

German spade in leather frame

GERMANY

Sergeant Telegraphist (Feldwebel)
German Infantry (North Italy)
1944-1945

Pistole M08 9 mm. Parabellum "Luger"

Pistole 38 (P38) Walther

German steel helmet
with camouflage cover
made of Italian material

German spade
in leather frame

GERMANY

Sergeant (Feldwebel)
"Feldpolizei"
1943-1945

Kar. 98k

Pistole M08 9 mm. Parabellum "Luger"

Pistole 38 (P38) Walther

Captured Wz/35 "Vis Radom"
Polish Browning (German markings)

Field cap M43 of the Feldpolizei
with German police emblem

Helmet M42
of the Feldpolizei

Water bottle issued to the Army,
Navy, Airforce and Party Units

German waterbottle
with bakelite drinking glass

Bayonet with troddel (dragon)
of the Feldpolizei

7.92 mm. Mauser
ammunition

95

GERMANY

Corporal (Obergefreiter)
German Infantry Regiment No. 67
Battle of the Bulge 1944

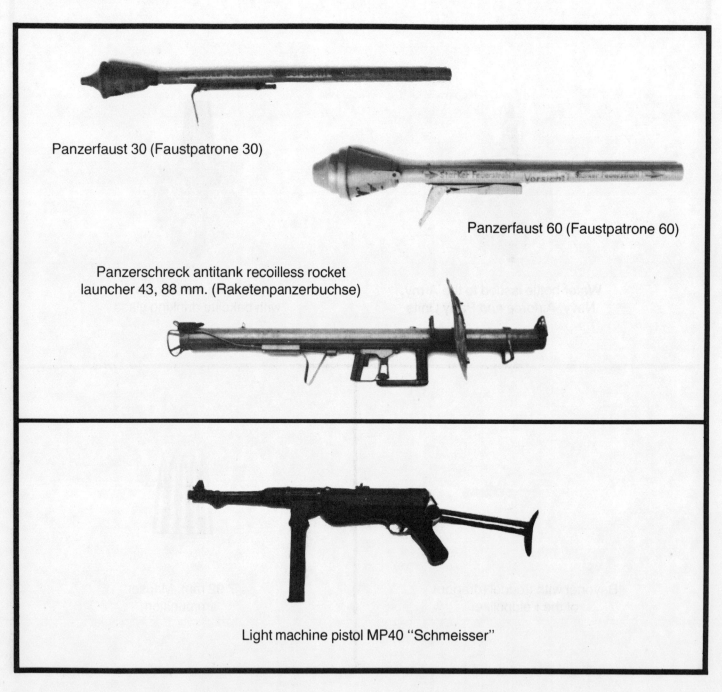

Panzerfaust 30 (Faustpatrone 30)

Panzerfaust 60 (Faustpatrone 60)

Panzerschreck antitank recoilless rocket
launcher 43, 88 mm. (Raketenpanzerbuchse)

Light machine pistol MP40 "Schmeisser"

M42 steel helmet
painted white
by the Germans
in Bastogne 1944

German water bottles
with different bakelite drinking glasses

German gas masks and metal gas mask box

3 types of German bayonets
used in the last year of the war

German spade
in leather frame

GERMANY

Corporal 1st Class (Hauptgefreiter)
German Coast Artillery
1939-1944

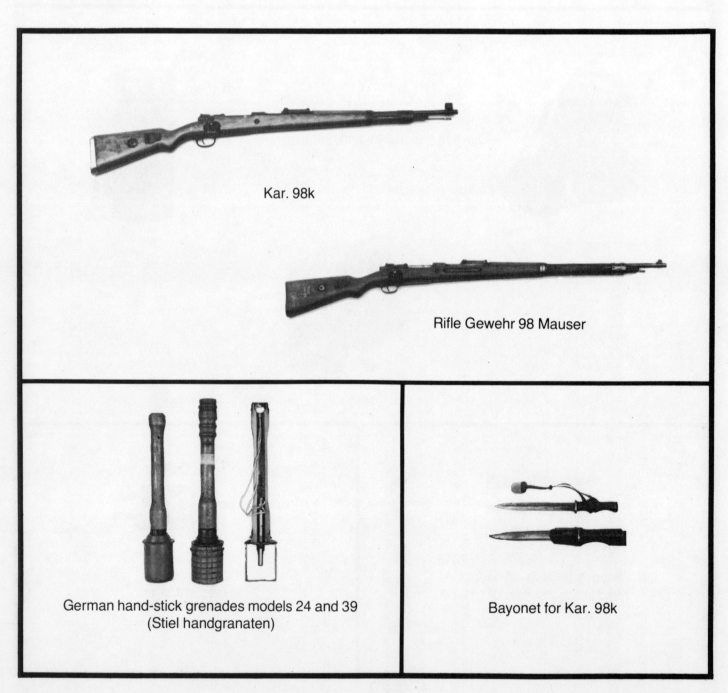

Kar. 98k

Rifle Gewehr 98 Mauser

German hand-stick grenades models 24 and 39
(Stiel handgranaten)

Bayonet for Kar. 98k

M43 Field cap
of the Wehrmacht
(Einheitsmütze)

German M38 Side cap (Feldmütze)

German Steel helmet M42

3 types of water bottles
issued to the Army,
Navy, Airforce and Party units

German water bottle
with bakelite drinking glass

German water bottle designed for
the Afrika Korps
uséd also in Italy
and was also issued
in the last year of
the war to Army units

German spade
in leather frame

7.92 mm. Mauser
ammunition

GERMANY

Private
German Infantry
Winter Uniform Eastern Front
1942-1944

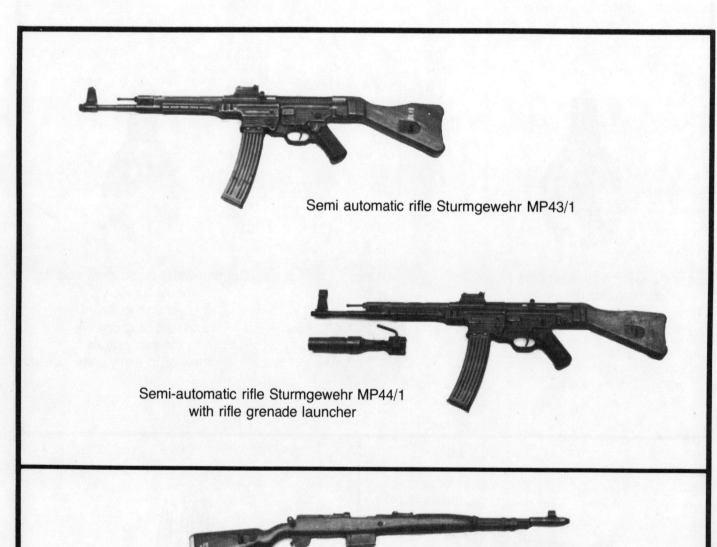

Semi automatic rifle Sturmgewehr MP43/1

Semi-automatic rifle Sturmgewehr MP44/1
with rifle grenade launcher

Gewehr 41(m) rifle specially made for cold weather,
note special trigger

German steel helmet M42
painted white in Russia

German water bottles

German gas masks and gas mask box

German offensive hand grenades

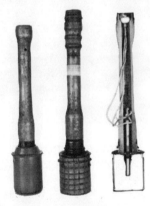

German hand-stick grenades
models 24 and 39

German spade in leather frame

7.92 mm. Mauser
ammunition

7.92 mm. Kurz 43
(short) ammunition

GERMANY

Sergeant Major (Oberscharführer)
Waffen SS Regiment
Leibstandarte Adolf Hitler

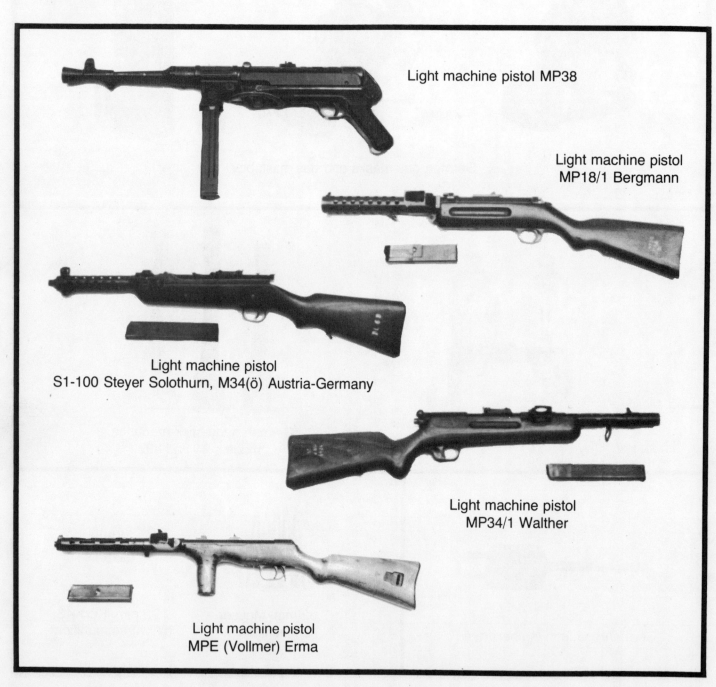

Light machine pistol MP38

Light machine pistol
MP18/1 Bergmann

Light machine pistol
S1-100 Steyer Solothurn, M34(ö) Austria-Germany

Light machine pistol
MP34/1 Walther

Light machine pistol
MPE (Vollmer) Erma

Kar. 98k

Steel helmet M35
of the Waffen SS

German Water bottle
issued to Party units

German gas masks and metal gas mask box

German hand-stick grenades
models 24 and 39

7.92 mm. Mauser
ammunition

GERMANY

Soldier Waffen SS
armed with a Panzerschreck
1944-1945

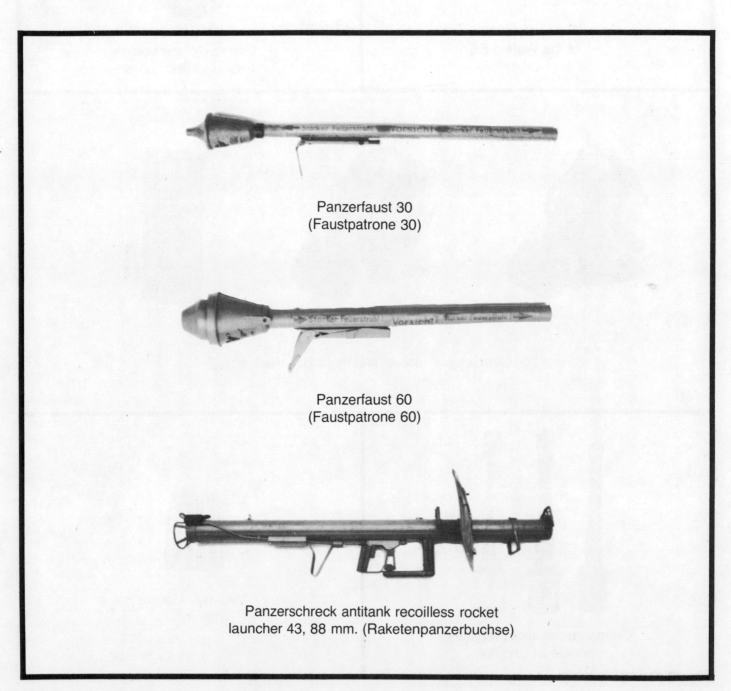

Panzerfaust 30
(Faustpatrone 30)

Panzerfaust 60
(Faustpatrone 60)

Panzerschreck antitank recoilless rocket
launcher 43, 88 mm. (Raketenpanzerbuchse)

MP43/1 Sturmgewehr

Rifle Gewehr 43 (Kar. 43)

Rifle Gewehr 41(w)
Selbstlade gewehr

Field cap M43
of the Waffen SS
dead-head insignia on the front
SS eagle on the left side

Steel helmet M35
of the Waffen SS

M42 of the Waffen SS
with 1st model cover

German bakelite water bottles

Two types of German gas masks
and metal gas mask box

German offensive hand grenade

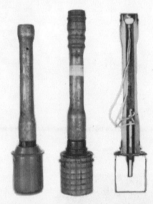

German hand-stick grenades models 24 and 39
(Stiel handgranaten)

Several types of bayonets
issued to the Wehrmacht
in the last year of the war

German/Czechoslovakian 7.92 mm.
Mauser ammunition

7.92 mm. Mauser
ammunition

7.92 mm. Kurz 43 (short)
ammunition

GERMANY

Sergeant (Wachtmeister)
German Antiaircraft Artillery (Flak)
1939-1945

Pistole M08 9 mm. Parabellum "Luger"

Pistole 38 (P38) Walther

M42 Luftwaffe helmet

M35 Luftwaffe helmet

Water bottle
issued to the Luftwaffe

Gas masks and gas mask box painted grey-blue
for the Luftwaffe

GERMANY

Soldier with Panzerfaust
German Infantry
1944-1945

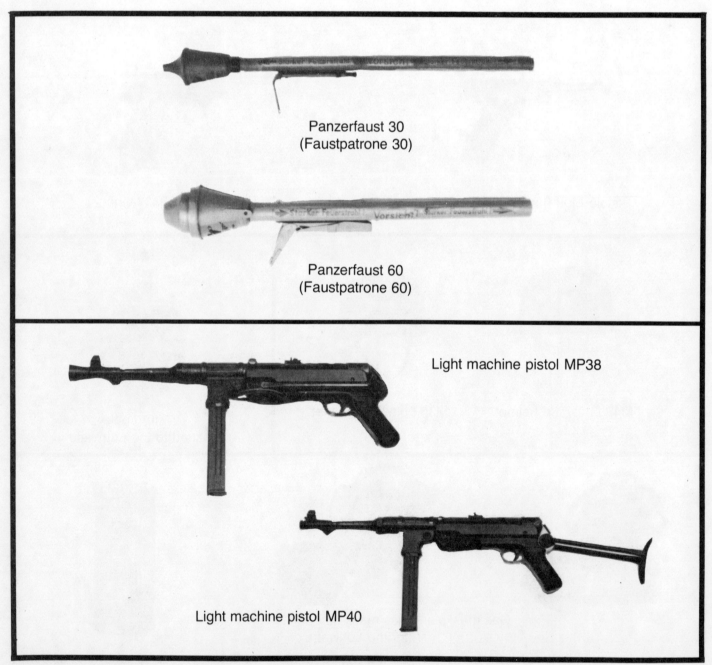

Panzerfaust 30
(Faustpatrone 30)

Panzerfaust 60
(Faustpatrone 60)

Light machine pistol MP38

Light machine pistol MP40

VG1-5 Versuchgerät or
Volkssturm Gewehr

MP43/1 Sturmgewehr

Gewehr 43 (Kar. .43)

Gewehr 98 Mauser

Gewehr 41(w)

German Steel helmet M42
with self-made helmet wirecover

German M43 field cap
(Einheitsmütze)

5 types of German water bottles
used in the last year of the war

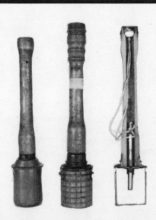

German offensive
hand grenade

German hand-stick grenade
models 24 and 39 (Stiel handgranaten)

German gas masks
and metal gas mask box

3 types of German
"Ersatz" bayonets

German spade
in leather frame

7.92 mm. Mauser ammunition

7.92 mm. Kurz 43 (short)
ammunition

GERMANY

1st Lieutenant
German Luftwaffe
1940

Pistole Sauer's modell 38H

German pilot cap of a Stuka pilot

GERMANY

German Prisoner (SchutzHaftling)
German concentration camp
1934-1945

Member of the S.A.
(Sturmabteilung) of the NSDAP
1926-1945

Pistole Sauer's modell 38H

German cap of the S.A.
brown with the Party eagle

GREAT BRITAIN

Major
Parachute Regiment
Normandy, Arnhem,
Greece, Rhine crossings
1944-1945

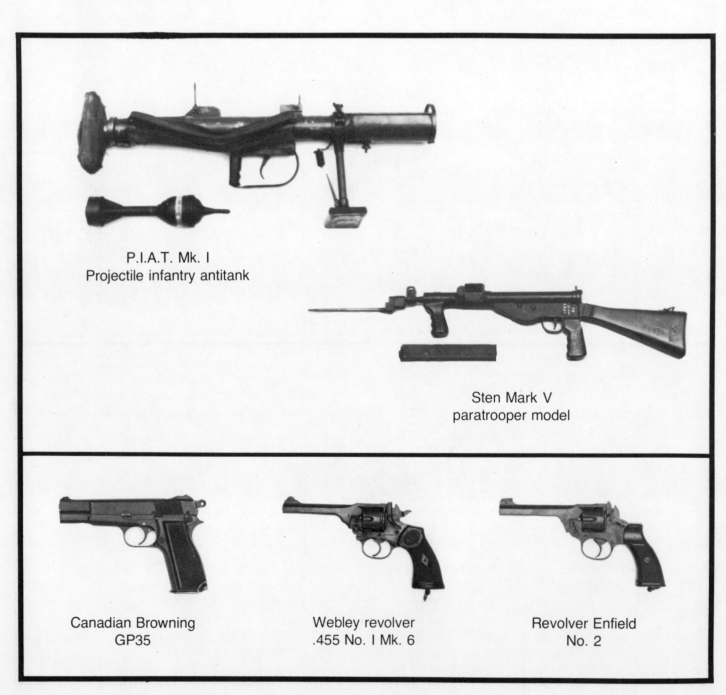

P.I.A.T. Mk. I
Projectile infantry antitank

Sten Mark V
paratrooper model

Canadian Browning
GP35

Webley revolver
.455 No. I Mk. 6

Revolver Enfield
No. 2

British paratrooper helmet
A.T. Mk. I 1943

British beret of
the parachute regiment

British blue enameled water bottle
1st model webbing frame   2nd model webbing frame

British smoke grenade

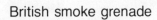

British No. 36M Mills grenade
offensive/defensive

British No. 69 Mk. I
offensive hand grenade (bakelite)

British 2nd model
gas mask

British 2nd model
gas mask bag

British trenching
tool equipment
in 2 parts

GREAT BRITAIN

Private 1st Class
Coldstream Guards
B.E.F. (British Expeditionary Forces)
Battle of Dunkirk
1940

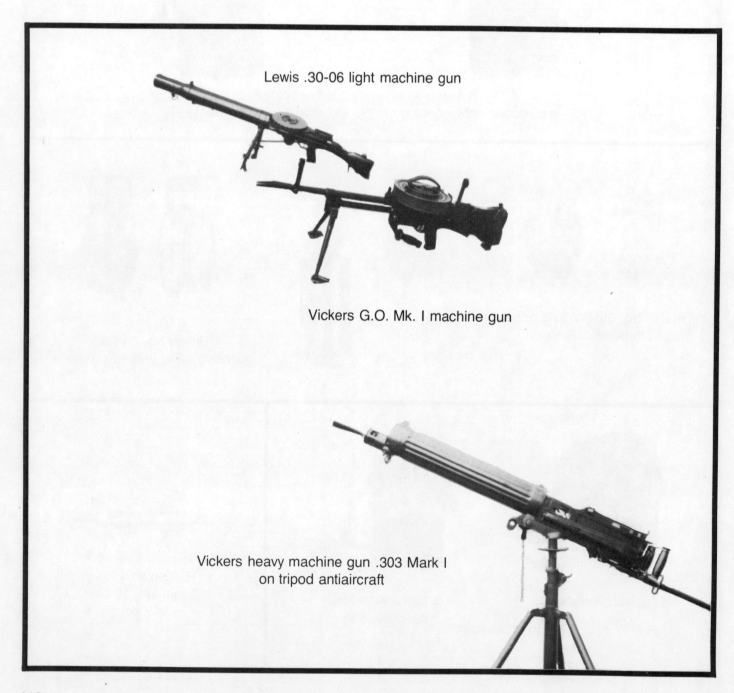

Lewis .30-06 light machine gun

Vickers G.O. Mk. I machine gun

Vickers heavy machine gun .303 Mark I
on tripod antiaircraft

American Thompson M 1928 A1 "Tommy-gun"

Lanchester Mark I

Rifle No. 1 Mk 3 Lee Enfield

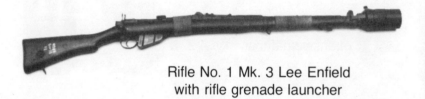

Rifle No. 1 Mk. 3 Lee Enfield
with rifle grenade launcher

Peaked cap
of the Guards Regiments

British steel helmet Mark II
with camouflage cover

British blue enameled water bottle
with 1st model webbing frame

British gas mask

1st model gas mask bag

British No. 36M Mills grenade
offensive/defensive

British smoke grenade

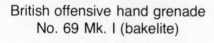

British offensive hand grenade
No. 69 Mk. I (bakelite)

English Bayonet No. I Mk. I

British trenching tool equipment
in 2 parts

.303 ammunition
for Lee Enfield

GREAT BRITAIN

Women's Health Service
Army Territorial Service
1940-1945

Cap for the
Women's Army Auxilliary Corps

British helmet Mk. II

British water bottles with
blue enameled bottle

British gas mask and bag
1st model

British gas mask and bag
2nd model

1st model webbing frame

2nd model webbing frame

GREAT BRITAIN

Private 1st Class (Lance-corporal)
Royal Signal Regiment
Campaign North-Africa, Italy
1942-1944

American Thompson M 1928 A1

Revolver Enfield No. 2

Webley revolver .455
No. 1 Mk. 6

Beret of the
Royal Signal Regiment

British steel helmet Mk. II

British water bottle with
blue enameled bottle
in 1st model webbing frame

British 1st model gas mask and gas mask bag

British No. 36M Mills grenade,
offensive/defensive

British smoke grenade

British No. 69 Mk. I
offensive hand grenade

British Commonwealth issued trenching
tool in 2 parts

.303 ammunition for Lee Enfield

GREAT BRITAIN

Corporal Scots Guards
(British 8th Army—Montgomery)
North Africa Campaign
1942-1943

Bren .303 Light machine gun with tripod mount

Bren .303 Light machine gun

British helmet Mk. II used in the desert
with first aid package

British water bottle with blue enameled bottle
in 1st model webbing frame

British No. 36M Mills grenade,
offensive/defensive

British smoke grenade

British No. 69 Mk. I
offensive hand grenade

British 1st model gas mask and gas mask bag

British trenching tool
in 2 parts

.303 ammunition for Lee Enfield

GREAT BRITAIN

Corporal
Queen's Royal Surrey Regiment
Winter 1944-1945

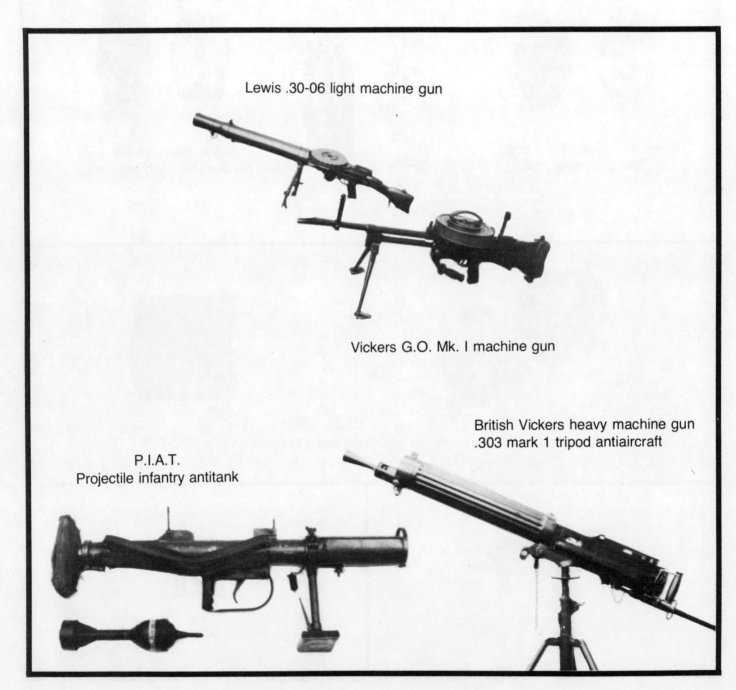

Lewis .30-06 light machine gun

Vickers G.O. Mk. I machine gun

British Vickers heavy machine gun
.303 mark 1 tripod antiaircraft

P.I.A.T.
Projectile infantry antitank

Light machine pistol Sten Mark II

Light machine pistol Sten Mark III

Rifle No. 1 Mk. 3 Lee Enfield

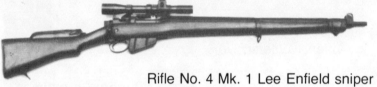

Rifle No. 4 Mk. 1 Lee Enfield sniper

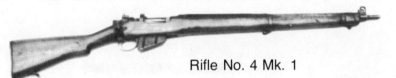

Rifle No. 4 Mk. 1

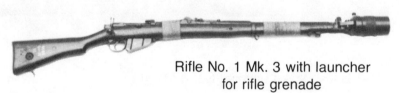

Rifle No. 1 Mk. 3 with launcher
for rifle grenade

Beret of the
Royal Surrey Regiment

British steel helmet Mk. II
with cover

British water bottle with
second model webbing frame

British gas mask 2nd model

British gas mask bag 2nd model

No. 36 M Mills grenade
offensive/defensive

Smoke grenade

No. 69 Mk. I
offensive grenade
(bakelite)

British spike bayonet No. 4 Mk. II

British bayonets Mk. II and I

British trenching tool
equipment in 2 parts

.303 ammunition Lee Enfield

GREAT BRITAIN

Pilot R.A.F.
Dutch Section
1940-1945

Webley revolver .455 No. I Mk. 6

Revolver Enfield No. 2

Officers peaked cap worn by
a Dutch officer in the R.A.F.

British pilot cap
for Spitfire pilots

HOLLAND

Private
Dutch Depot Battalions
"Vesting Holland"
May 1940

Lewis light machine gun
M20 6.5 mm.

Schwarzloze
heavy machine gun 6.5 mm.

Rifle M95 (Mannlicher)

Carbine M95 for artillery,
fortifications and engineers

Carbine M95 for military police
(Maréchaussée)

Pistol M24 (Belgian FN M22)

Dutch steel helmet M23
olive green painted with Dutch lion

Dutch water bottle
worn in the haversack

Dutch gas mask and gas mask bag

Dutch offensive hand grenade

Dutch offensive and
defensive hand grenade

Dutch bayonet M95 long model

6.5 mm. M95 ammunition

HOLLAND

Private 1st Class
Royal Dutch Brigade "Princess Irene"
Normandy, Belgium, Southern part
of the Netherlands
1944/45

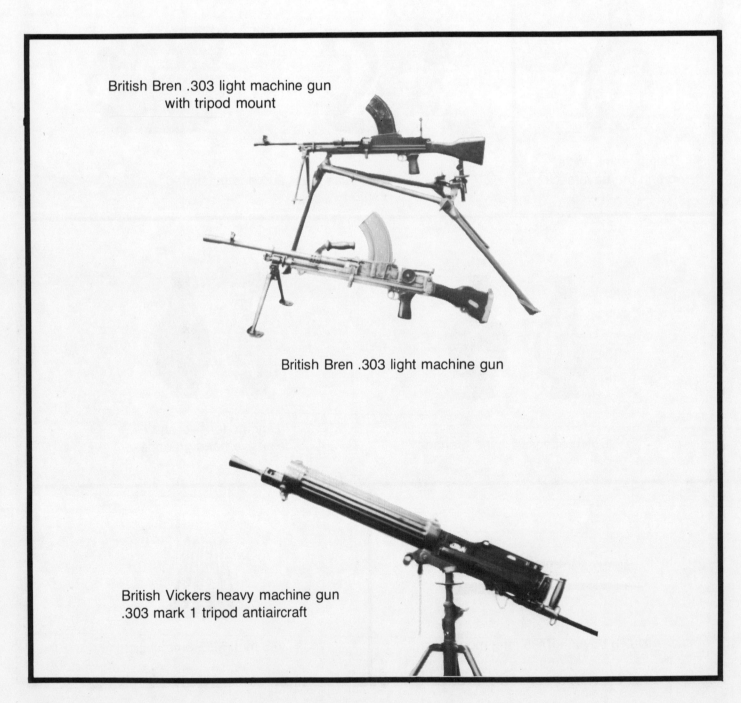

British Bren .303 light machine gun
with tripod mount

British Bren .303 light machine gun

British Vickers heavy machine gun
.303 mark 1 tripod antiaircraft

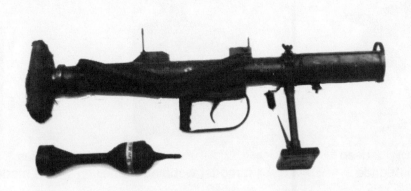

British P.I.A.T. Mk. I
Projectile infantry antitank

British No. I Mk. 3 Lee Enfield

British No. 4 Mk. 1 Lee Enfield Sniper

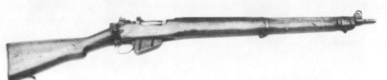

British No. 4 Mk. 1 Lee Enfield

British light machine gun
Sten Mark II

British helmet Mk. 2 used
in the Dutch brigade

British waterbottles
1st model webbing frame   2nd model webbing frame

British 2nd model gas mask and gas mask bag

British No. 36M Mills grenade
offensive/defensive

British smoke grenade

British No. 69 Mk. I
offensive hand grenade
(Bakelite)

British bayonet No. 4 Mk. III (spike)

British
.303 ammunition Lee Enfield

British trenching tool equipment

HOLLAND

Member of the WA
(Weerbaarheidsafdeling)
NSB (Nationalist Socialist Movement)
1932-1945

German pistole M08
9 mm. Parabellum "Luger"

Dutch M24 pistol
(FN modèle 1922 M22)

German pistole 38 (P38) Walther

German Sauer's modell 38H

Peaked cap of the WA of the NSB
cap manufactured in Nazi-style

HOLLAND

Officer Dutch Resistance
1944-1945

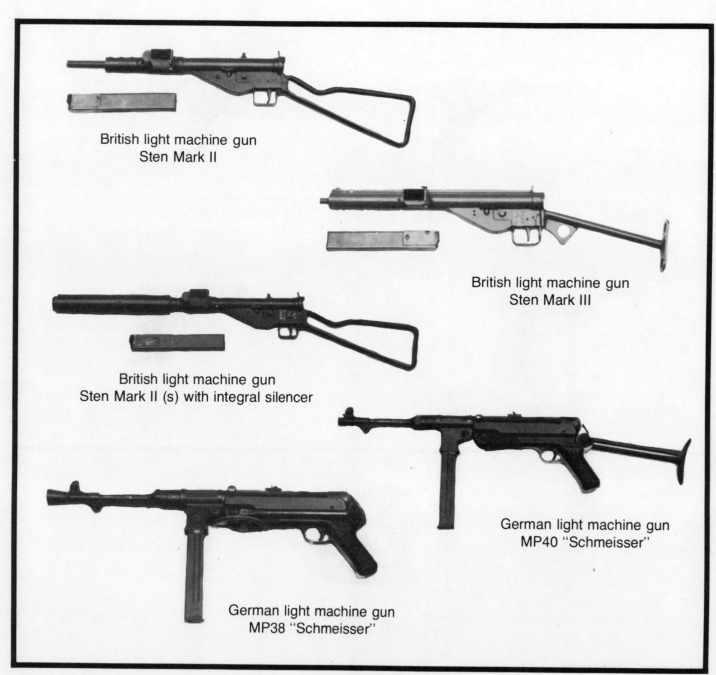

British light machine gun
Sten Mark II

British light machine gun
Sten Mark III

British light machine gun
Sten Mark II (s) with integral silencer

German light machine gun
MP40 "Schmeisser"

German light machine gun
MP38 "Schmeisser"

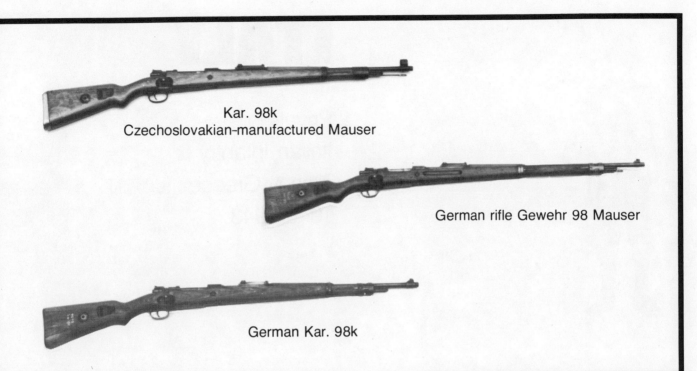

Kar. 98k
Czechoslovakian-manufactured Mauser

German rifle Gewehr 98 Mauser

German Kar. 98k

German pistole M. 08
9 mm. Parabellum "Luger"

Pistol M24
(Belgian-manufactured FN M22)

German Pistole 38 (P38)
Walther

German Pistole Sauer's modell 38H

Dutch steel helmet M24
painted black by the Resistance

German
7.92 mm. Mauser
ammunition

135

ITALY

Private
Italian Infantry
Albany-Greece
1940-1943

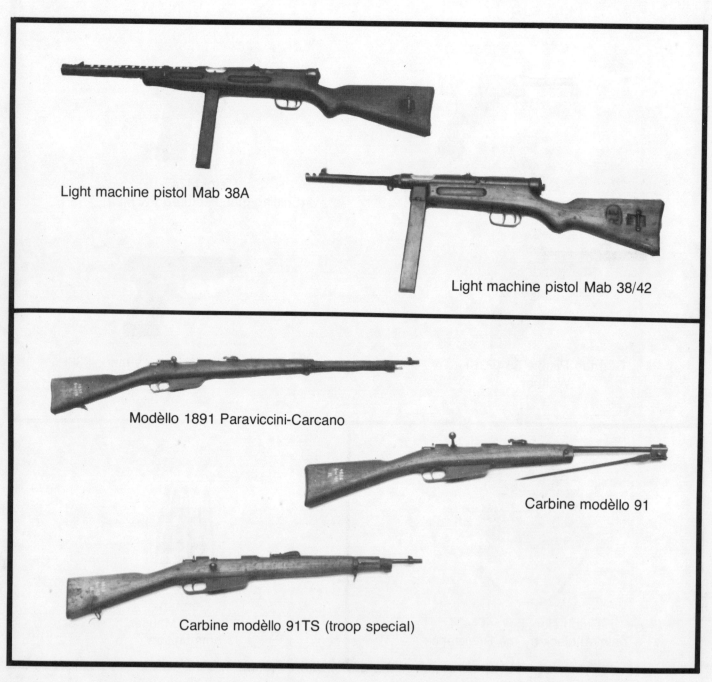

Light machine pistol Mab 38A

Light machine pistol Mab 38/42

Modèllo 1891 Paraviccini-Carcano

Carbine modèllo 91

Carbine modèllo 91TS (troop special)

Italian steel helmet
M 1935

Italian water bottle
with metal bottom cover

Italian gas mask

French gas mask bag and
gas mask captured by the Italians

Several types of
Italian bayonets M 1891

Clip with 6.5 mm.
Mannlicher-Carcano ammunition

ITALY

Soldier of the Student Battalion
Fascist Militia
North Africa Campaign
1940-1942

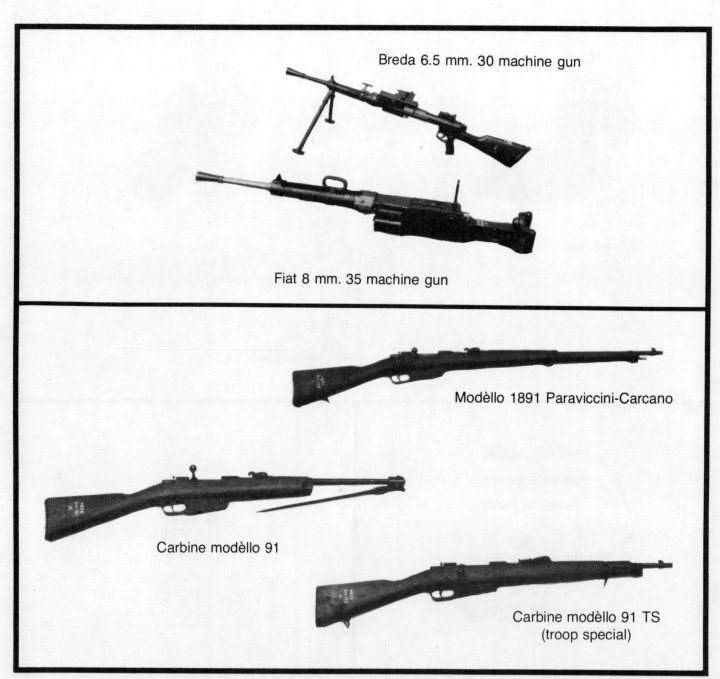

Breda 6.5 mm. 30 machine gun

Fiat 8 mm. 35 machine gun

Modèllo 1891 Paraviccini-Carcano

Carbine modèllo 91

Carbine modèllo 91 TS
(troop special)

Pistol Baretta 9 mm. short 1942
modèllo 1934

Italian sun helmet
made of cork

Small Italian water bottle

Italian gas mask

Captured French gas masks
used in the Italian army

3 types of Italian bayonets M 1891

6.5 mm. Mannlicher-Carcano
ammunition

ITALY

Soldier Bersaglieri
Russia and Africa
1939-1944

Rifle modèllo 1891
Paraviccini-Carcano

Pistol 1942 Baretta
9 mm. short modèllo 1934

Cockfeathered
Italian helmet M 1935
of the Bersaglieri

Large Italian water bottle
with metal bottom cover

Italian
offensive hand
grenades

Captured French gas mask
used in the Italian forces

3 types of Italian bayonets
M 1891

6.5 mm.
Mannlicher-Carcano
ammunition

JAPAN

Officer
in tropical uniform
Pacific Ocean
1941-1945

Pistol type 94 Shikikenju

Pistol model 14 (1925) Nambu

Samurai officers sword

Japanese field combat cap
with sun-protecting flaps
for tropical use

Japanese water bottle
for officers with
light brown leather strap

JAPAN

Light Machine Gunner 1st Class
Japanese Infantry
1942-1945

Hotchkiss heavy machine gun model 92

7.7 mm. light machine gun model 99 (1939)

Nambu 6.5 mm. 1922 light machine gun

6.5 mm. light machine gun model 96 (1936)
with fixed bayonet type Arisaka

Pistol model 14 (1925) Nambu

Pistol type 94 Shikikenju

Japanese steel helmet
model 1930-1932

2 types of Japanese water bottles
used in the Army

Japanese defensive hand grenade

Japanese defensive hand grenade

Japanese defensive hand grenade
model 91/1931

Japanese hand-stick grenade

Japanese gas mask

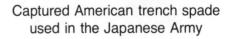

Captured American trench spade
used in the Japanese Army

JAPAN

Corporal
Japanese Infantry
1939-1945

Hotchkiss heavy machine gun model 92

7.7 mm. light machine gun model 99 (1939)

Nambu 6.5 mm. 1922 light machine gun

6.5 mm. light machine gun model 96 (1936)
with fixed bayonet type Arisaka

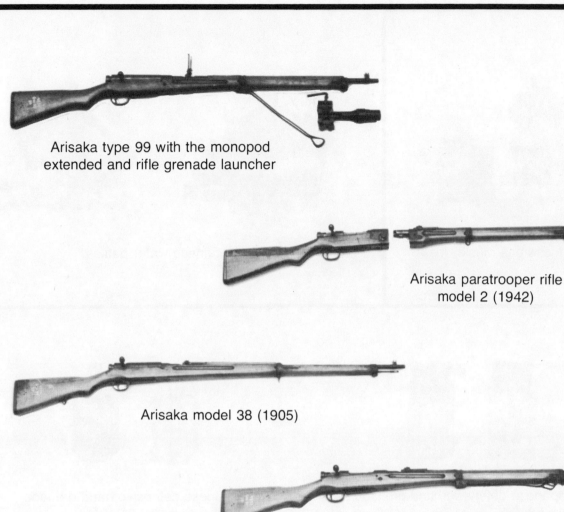

Arisaka type 99 with the monopod
extended and rifle grenade launcher

Arisaka paratrooper rifle
model 2 (1942)

Arisaka model 38 (1905)

Arisaka type 99

Carbine model 38 Arisaka

Japanese field cap

Japanese steel helmet
model 1930-1932
with cloth tropical cover

Japanese gas mask

Japanese water bottles

Japanese defensive hand grenade

Japanese defensive hand grenade
model 91/1931

Japanese defensive hand grenade

Japanese hand-stick grenade

Japanese bayonet
for Arisaka rifle
M99 (1939)

6.5 mm. Arisaka
ammunition

JAPAN

Soldier Japanese Infantry
Infiltration Groups
armed with knee-mortar
1941-1945

Japanese 50 mm. grenade
discharger model 89 (1929)

Nambu 6.5 mm. 1922 light machine gun

6.5 mm. light machine gun model 96 (1936)
with fixed bayonet type Arisaka

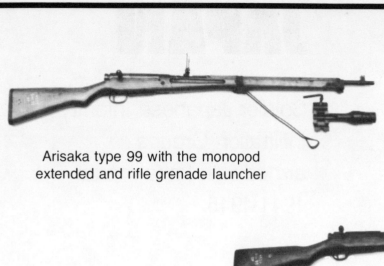

Arisaka type 99 with the monopod
extended and rifle grenade launcher

Arisaka model 38 (1905)

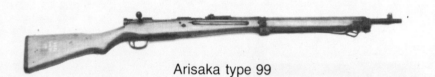

Arisaka type 99

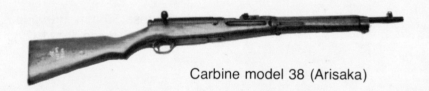

Carbine model 38 (Arisaka)

Japanese field cap

Japanese field cap

Japanese steel helmet
model 1930-1932

Japanese gas mask

Japanese water bottles

Japanese defensive hand grenade

Japanese defensive hand grenade
model 91/1931

Japanese defensive hand grenade

Japanese hand-stick grenade

Captured American spade
used in
the Japanese forces

6.5 mm. Arisaka ammunition

POLAND

Soldier
1st Polish People's Army
1944-1945

Russian light machine gun
PPD 1940

Mosin Nagant carbine
manufactured in Poland

Polish field cap
with Polish eagle

Russian Pistolet obr 1930g/1933g
TT (Tul 'skiy Tokarev)
Tokarev

Russian Revolver Sistemy
Nagana obr 1895g
Nagant M 1895

Pistol W2/35 Vis Radom
Polish Browning

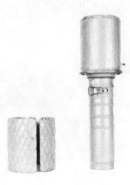

Russian hand-stick grenade
(offensive/defensive)
Granata obr R.G.D. 33

German spade in Russian frame

POLAND

Private
Polish Army
1939

Polish Browning 1917 machine gun
CKMw2.30

B.A.R. 7.92 mm.
Polish manufactured

Mosin Nagant carbine
Polish manufactured

German Kar. 98k

Pistol W2/35 Vis Radom
Polish Browning

Polish steel helmet
M 1936

Polish Mauser bayonet
also used in Rumania

German 7.92 Mauser
ammunition

RUMANIA

Corporal
8th Rumanian Infantry Regiment
as German ally 1941-1945
as Russian ally 1945

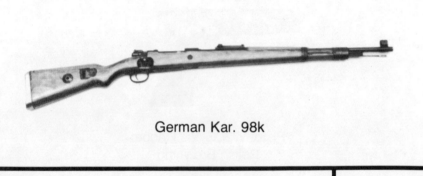

German Kar. 98k

Helmet M 1923
designed and manufactured
in Holland
for the Rumanian Army

Rumanian
field cap

Rumanian enameled
water bottle

Rumanian bayonet for Kar. 98k

Rumanian 6.5 mm. ammunition

USA

Technical Sergeant
3rd US Infantry Division
3rd US Army (General Patton)
1943 Invasion Sicily/Battles in Italy

Browning .30 1919 A4 air cooled

Browning .30 1917 and
1917 A1 machine gun water cooled

Thompson M1A1 "Tommy" gun

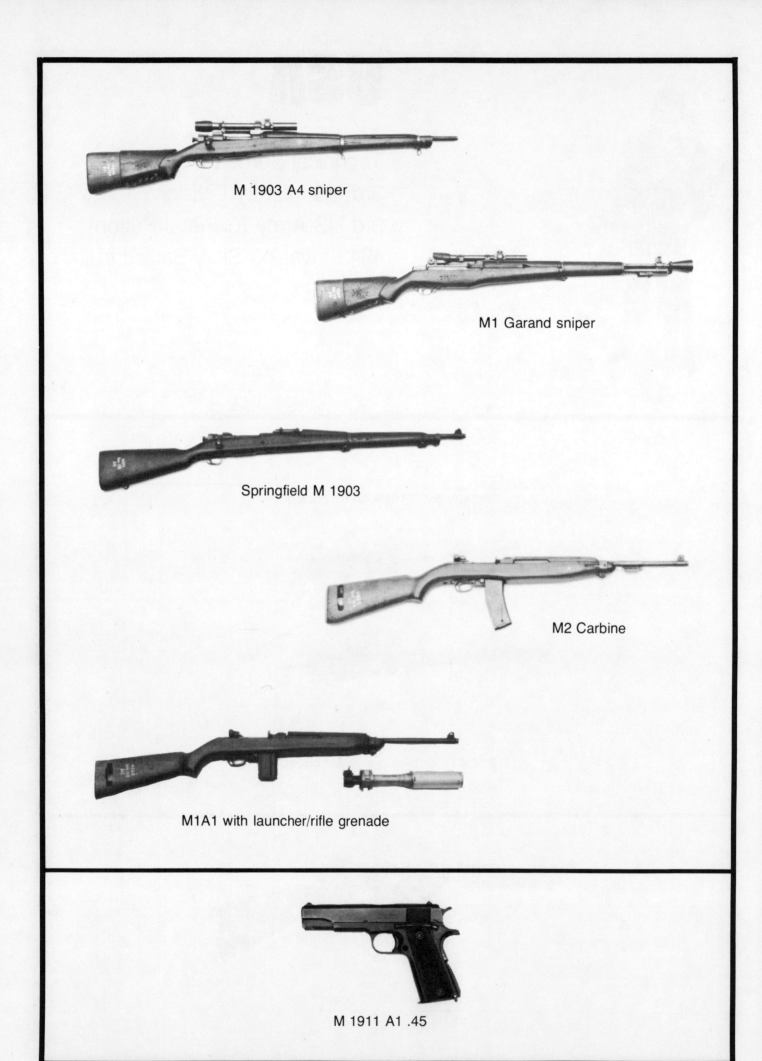

M 1903 A4 sniper

M1 Garand sniper

Springfield M 1903

M2 Carbine

M1A1 with launcher/rifle grenade

M 1911 A1 .45

American steel helmet M1

American woolen jeep cap

American water bottle

American Mk. 2A1
fragmentation grenade defensive

American smoke grenade

American trenching tool

American tool in 2 parts 1943

.30-06 Garand
ammunition

.30-06 Springfield
ammunition

.30 carbine M1
ammunition

American bayonet M1

USA

Private 1st Class
7th American Armored Division
(1st Army General Hodges)
Battle of the Bulge
1944

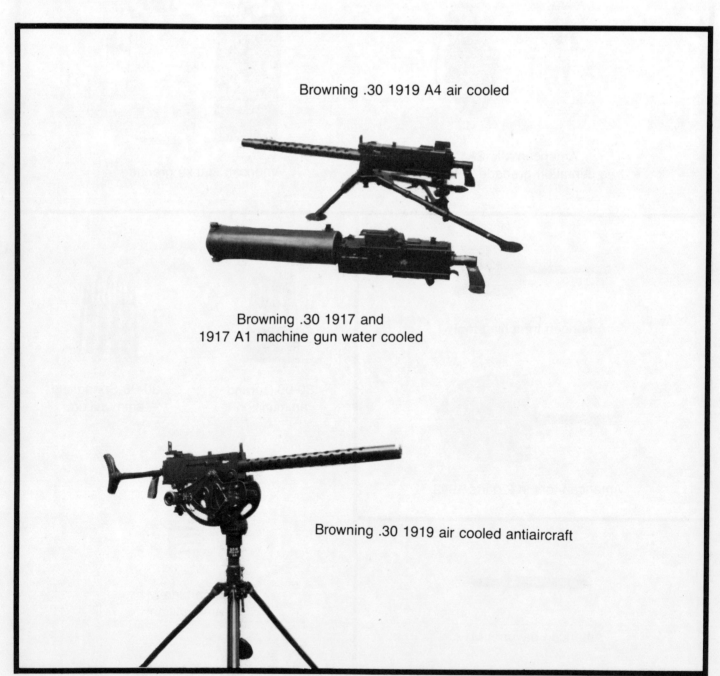

Browning .30 1919 A4 air cooled

Browning .30 1917 and
1917 A1 machine gun water cooled

Browning .30 1919 air cooled antiaircraft

Browning automatic rifle 1918 A2 B.A.R.

Browning .50 heavy machine gun M2

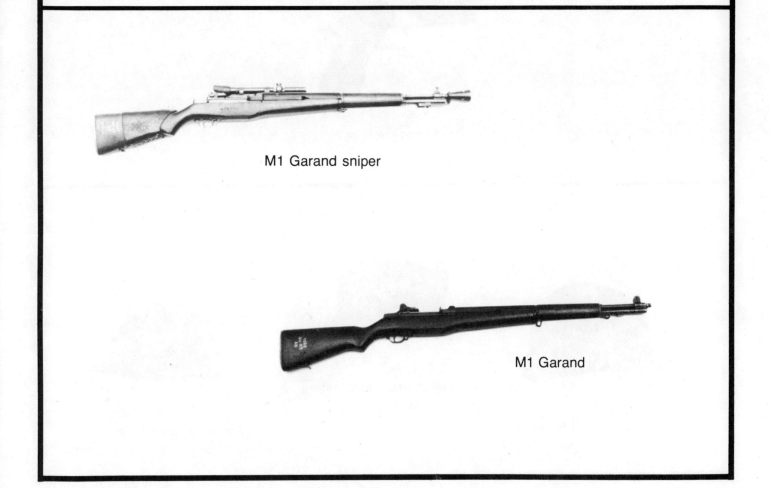

M1 Garand sniper

M1 Garand

M2 carbine

M1A1 with launcher/rifle grenade

M 1911 A1 .45

American standard issued
fatigue cap

American steel helmet M1

American woolen jeep cap

American water bottle

American water bottle

Mk. 2A1
fragmentation grenade defensive

American smoke
hand grenade

American trenching tool

.30-06 Garand
ammunition

.30-06 Springfield
ammunition

American bayonet M1

.30 carbine M1
ammunition

USA

Paratrooper
Operation "Market Garden"
Holland
1944

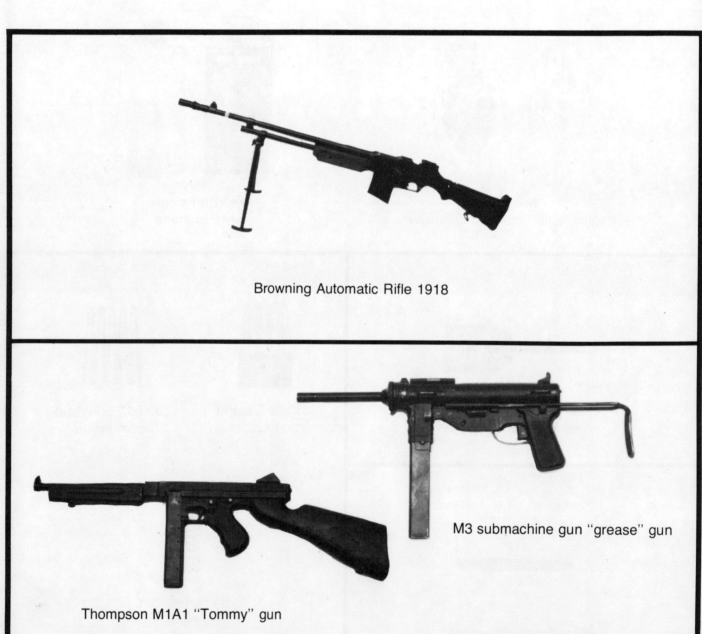

Browning Automatic Rifle 1918

Thompson M1A1 "Tommy" gun

M3 submachine gun "grease" gun

M1A1 carbine

M 1911 A1 .45

American steel helmet
paratrooper model M1
with special parastrap

American standard issued
fatigue cap

American water bottles

.30-06 Garand
ammunition

.30-06 Springfield
ammunition

USA

Sergeant with Bazooka
2nd US Infantry Division (Indianhead)
Normandy
1944

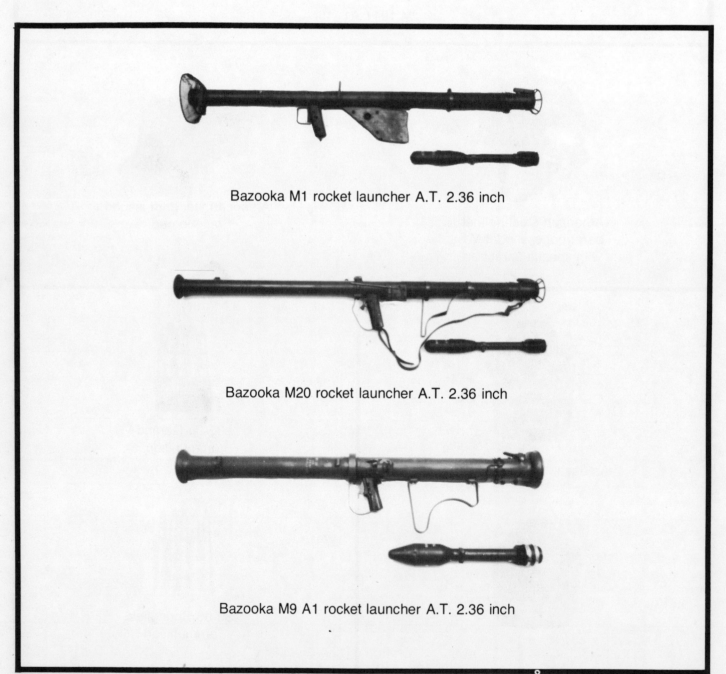

Bazooka M1 rocket launcher A.T. 2.36 inch

Bazooka M20 rocket launcher A.T. 2.36 inch

Bazooka M9 A1 rocket launcher A.T. 2.36 inch

Browning .30 1919 A4 air cooled

Browning .30 1917 and
1917 A1 machine gun water cooled

Thompson M1A1 "Tommy" gun

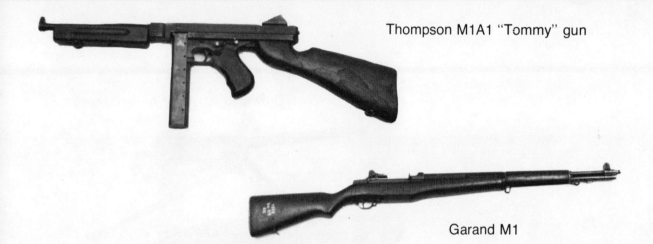

Garand M1

American steel helmet
with cover

American standard issued
fatigue cap

American Mk. 2A1
fragmentation grenade defensive

American smoke grenade

.30-06 Garand
ammunition

USA

Marine, USMC
Battle in the Pacific
1943-1945

Browning .30 1919 A4 air cooled

Browning .30 1917 and
1917 A1 machine gun water cooled

Browning .30 machine rifle M 1918 A2 B

Johnson light machine gun 1941

Browning .50 heavy machine gun M2

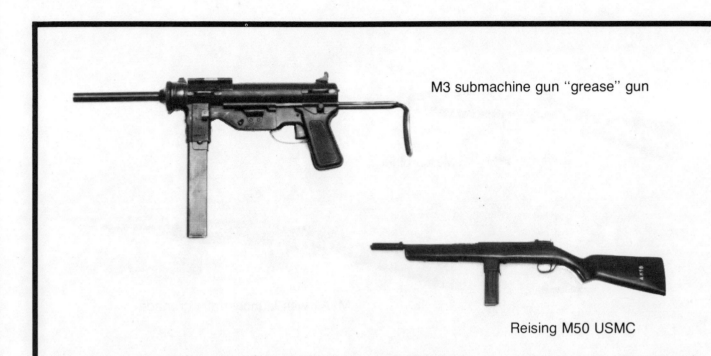

M3 submachine gun "grease" gun

Reising M50 USMC

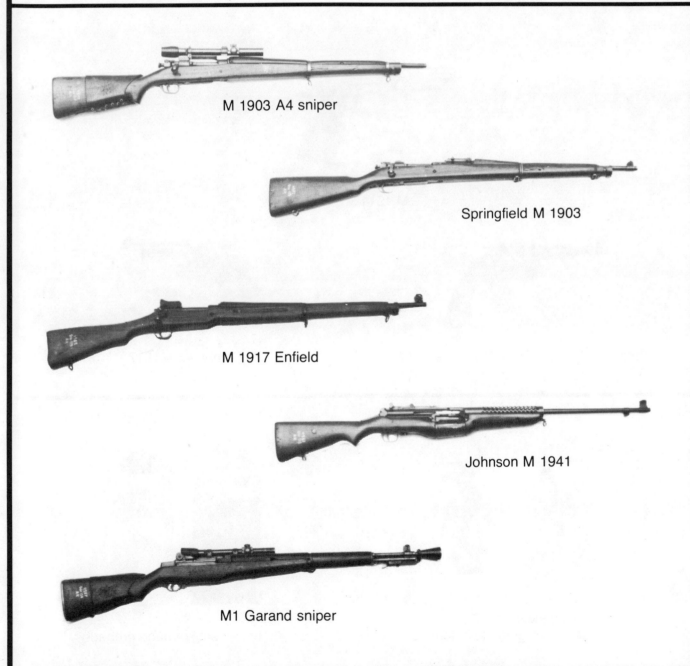

M 1903 A4 sniper

Springfield M 1903

M 1917 Enfield

Johnson M 1941

M1 Garand sniper

M2 carbine

M1A1 with launcher/rifle grenade

M 1911 A1 .45

Smith and Wesson No. 2 revolver 1917

Colt army .45 M1917

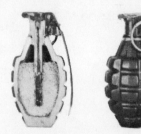

American Mk. 2A1
fragmentation grenade defensive

American smoke hand grenade

American steel helmet M1
with jungle tropic cover,
mosquito net

American standard issued
fatigue cap

American water bottle

American water bottle

American trenching tool

.30-06 Garand
ammunition

American trenching tool
in 2 parts 1943

.30-06 Springfield
ammunition

USSR

Sergeant of the Guard—Infantry
Summer Uniform
1943-1945

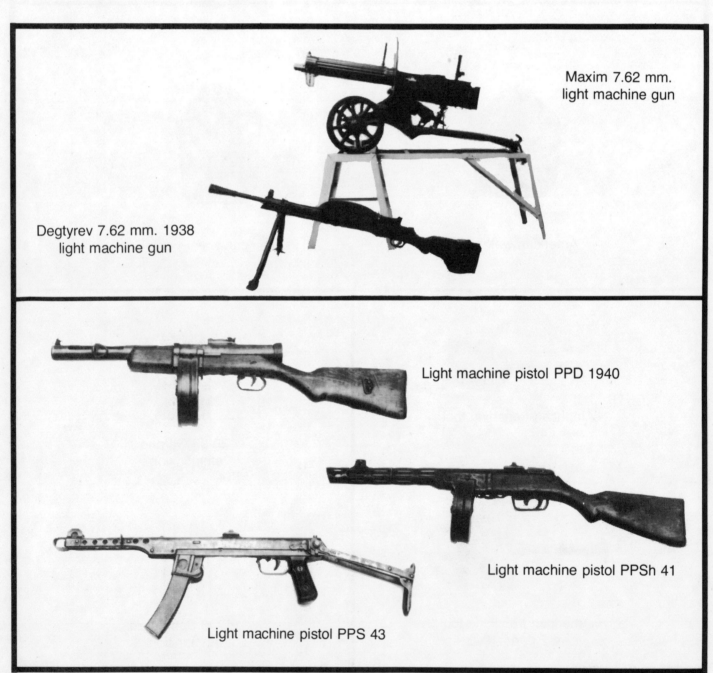

Maxim 7.62 mm.
light machine gun

Degtyrev 7.62 mm. 1938
light machine gun

Light machine pistol PPD 1940

Light machine pistol PPSh 41

Light machine pistol PPS 43

Semi-automatic rifle
SVT40, Samozary Adnayal
Vintovka Tokareva obr 1940g

Rifle M 1891/08, 3 Lineyaya
Vintovka obr 1891g

Mosin Nagant 3 Lineynyi
Karabin obr 1910g Nagant

Mosin Nagant Karabin
obr 1944g Nagant

Mosin Nagant "Made in Poland"

Pistolet obr 1930g/1933g TT
(Tul 'skiy Tokarev) TT30

Revolver Sistemy Nagana
obr 1895g (Nagant M 1895)

Russian steel helmet of the
(M 1940) Guard Infantry of Moscow

Russian water bottle

Russian gas mask

Russian hand grenades

Granata Marki F.I.
(Russian offensive grenade)

Russian hand-stick grenade
(offensive/defensive)
Granata obr R.G.D.

Russian bayonet Schtuyk
obr 1891

7.62 mm.
Mosin Nagant ammunition

Russian trenching tool spade

USSR

Soldier
Russian Infantry
Winter Uniform
1941-1944

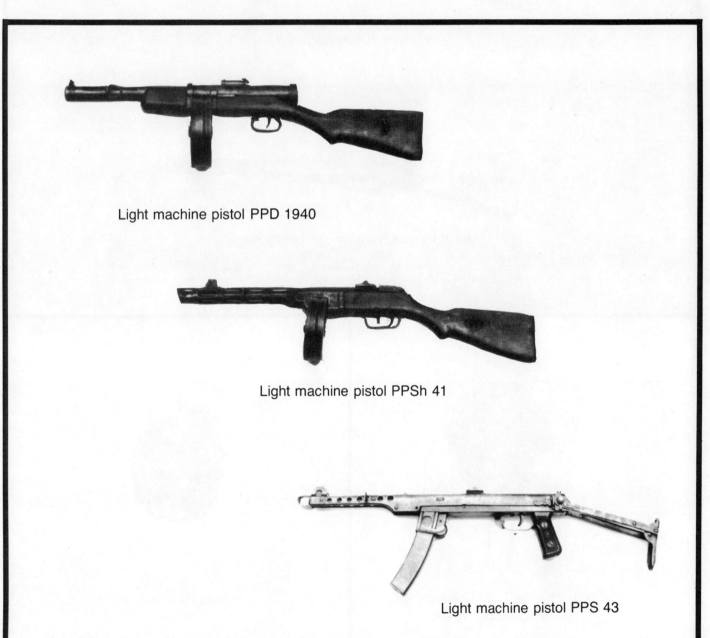

Light machine pistol PPD 1940

Light machine pistol PPSh 41

Light machine pistol PPS 43

Rifle M 1891/08, 3 Lineyaya
Vintovka obr 1891g

Mosin Nagant 3 Lineynyi Karabin
obr 1910g Nagant

Mosin Nagant Karabin obr 1944g Nagant

Russian fur hat in combination with
helmet model 1940

Russian water bottle

Russian gas mask

Russian hand grenades

Granata Marki F.I.
(Russian offensive grenade)

Russian hand-stick grenade
offensive/defensive
Granata obr R.G.D. 33

Captured German tool used in the
Russian Army in Russian frame

Russian spade in leather frame

Russian bayonet
Schtuyk obr 1891

7.62 mm.
Mosin Nagant ammunition

USSR

Junior Sergeant
Russian Infantry
Winter Uniform
1943-1945

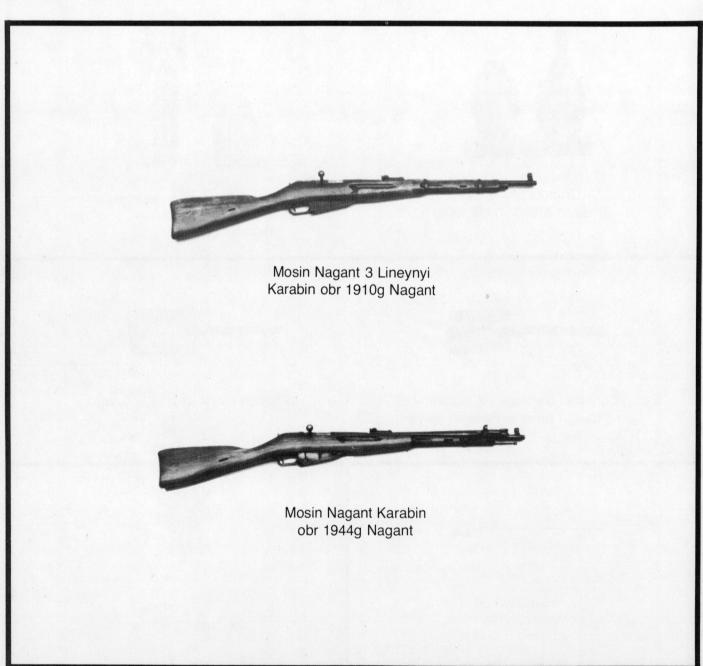

Mosin Nagant 3 Lineynyi
Karabin obr 1910g Nagant

Mosin Nagant Karabin
obr 1944g Nagant

Fur hat with red star Soviet emblem

Russian water bottle

Russian gas mask

Granata Marki F.I.
(Russian offensive grenade)

Russian hand-stick grenade
offensive/defensive
Granata obr R.G.D. 33

Captured German spade

Russian bayonet
Schtuyk obr 1891

7.62 mm.
Mosin Nagant ammunition

USSR

Private
Russian Guard
Infantry
Autumn Uniform
1941-1945

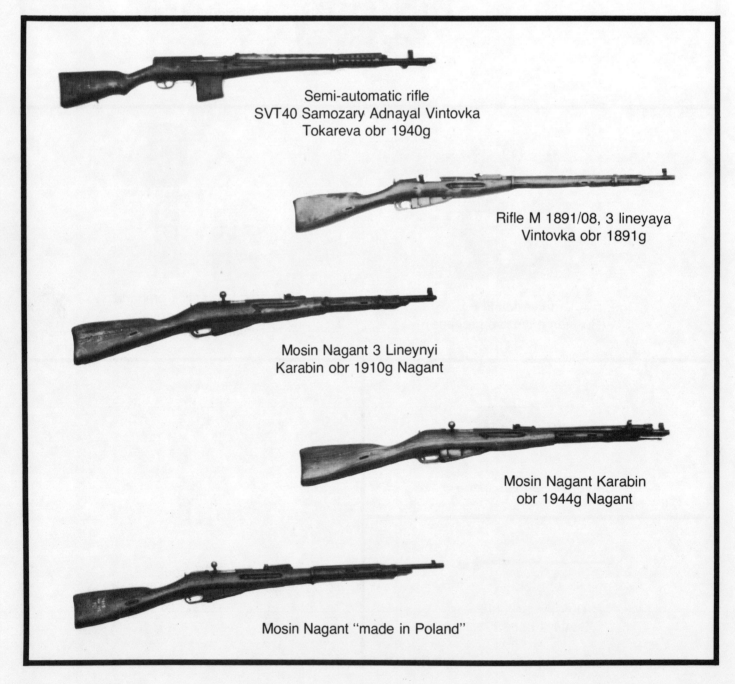

Semi-automatic rifle
SVT40 Samozary Adnayal Vintovka
Tokareva obr 1940g

Rifle M 1891/08, 3 lineyaya
Vintovka obr 1891g

Mosin Nagant 3 Lineynyi
Karabin obr 1910g Nagant

Mosin Nagant Karabin
obr 1944g Nagant

Mosin Nagant "made in Poland"

Russian steel helmet
M 1936

Russian water bottle

Russian gas mask

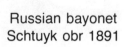

Russian bayonet
Schtuyk obr 1891

7.62 mm.
Mosin Nagant ammunition

USSR

Private
Siberian contingents
Autumn Uniform
1941-1945

Light machine pistol PPD 1940

Light machine pistol PPSh 41

Fur hat worn by
the Siberian contingents

Granata Marki F.I.
(Russian offensive grenade)

Russian hand-stick grenade
(offensive/defensive)
Granata obr R.G.D.

Russian water bottle

Captured German spade
in Russian frame

USSR

Woman soldier
Military Police Traffic
1942-1945 Berlin

Mosin Nagant 3 Lineynyi Karabin
obr 1910g Nagant

Side cap worn by
military traffic police women
in Berlin 1945

7.62 mm.
Mosin Nagant ammunition

YUGOSLAVIA

Woman Freedom Fighter (Partisan)
Resistance Army under Tito
1941-1944

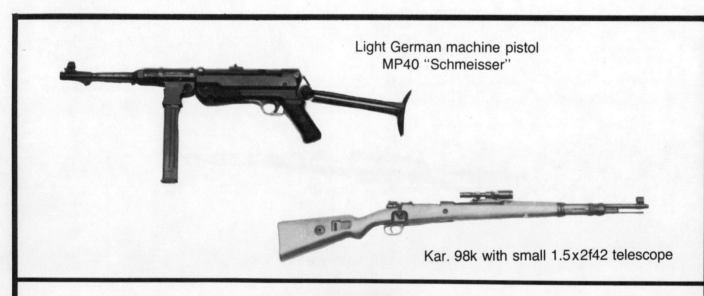

Light German machine pistol
MP40 "Schmeisser"

Kar. 98k with small 1.5×2f42 telescope

Yugoslavian side cap with
communist red star emblem of Tito's troops

German water bottle

German
7.92 mm. Mauser
ammunition

German
7.92 mm. Mauser
Kurz 43 (short) ammunition

TANKS
MORTARS
SMALL FIELD GUNS

German cable controlled
demolition vehicle Goliath-B1

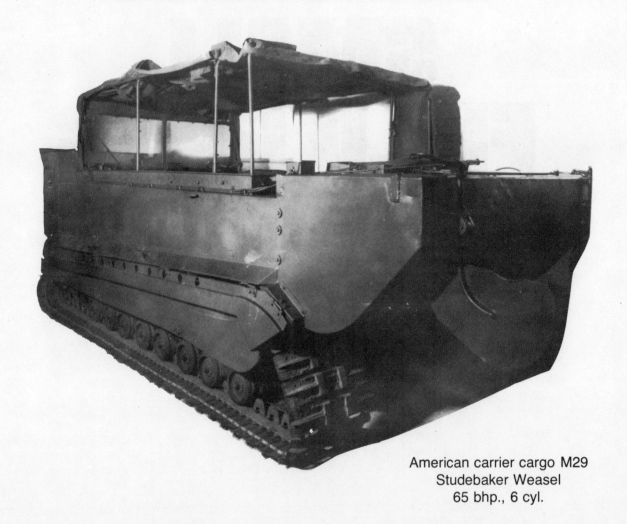

American carrier cargo M29
Studebaker Weasel
65 bhp., 6 cyl.

French tank H35 Hotchkiss
17 mph. 37 mm. gun, 1 machine gun

Japanese light tank
Tankette model 2597 (1937)
28 mph., with machine gun

MORTARS

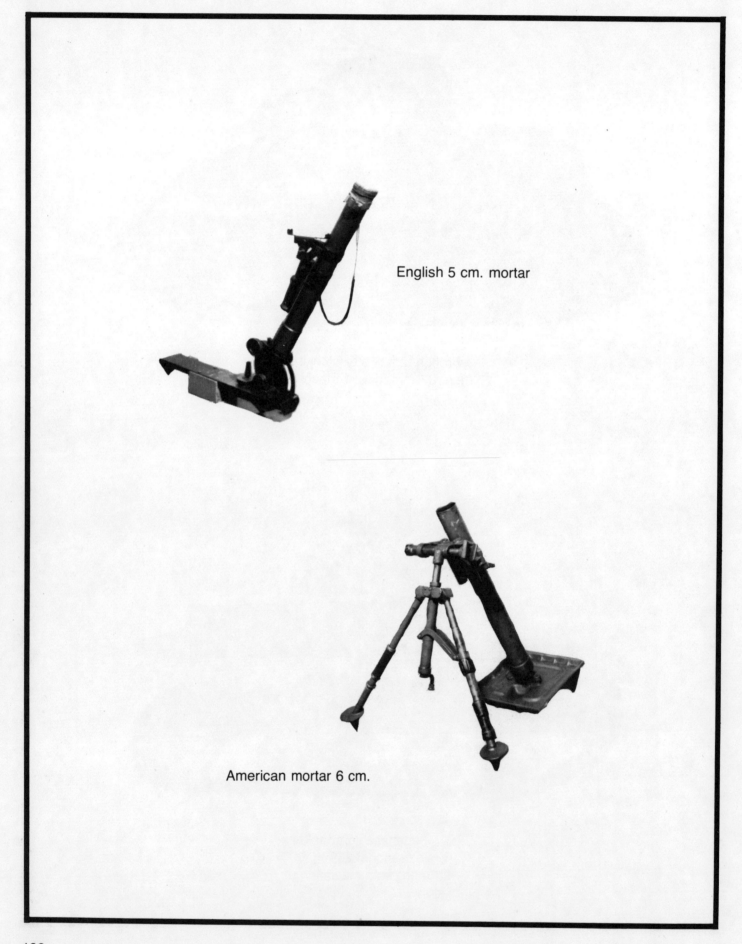

English 5 cm. mortar

American mortar 6 cm.

French mortar Mle. 37, 5 cm.

German 5 cm. light mortar (Granatwerfer 36)
5 cm. GrW36)

Russian light infantry mortar 5 cm.

SMALL FIELD GUNS

Japanese 70 mm. battalion howitzer Type 92 1932
with spoked artillery wheels

German four 20 mm. antiaircraft gun
of the Flak

German Raketenwerfer 43 Püppchen
made by Wasag Reinsdorf

German 75 mm. light infantry gun M18
with spoked artillery wheels

Russian howitzer with very short barrel

189

INDEX

HOLLAND

Ammunition: 69, 71, 129, 132, 135
Antitank guns: 131
Bayonets: 69, 71, 129, 132
Caps: 133
Carbines: 128
Field rifles: 68, 128, 131, 135
Gas masks: 69, 71, 129, 132
Gas mask bags: 69, 71, 129, 131
Grenades: 68, 70, 129, 132
Helmets: 69, 71, 129, 132, 135, 154
Light machine pistols: 131, 134
Machine guns: 70, 128, 130
Pistols: 129, 132, 135
Trenching tools: 132
Uniforms: 37, 38, 128, 130, 133, 134
Water bottles: 129, 132

ITALY

Ammunition: 137, 139, 140
Bayonets: 137, 139, 140
Carbines: 136, 138
Field rifles: 136, 138, 140
Gas masks: 137, 139, 140
Gas mask bags: 137, 139, 140
Grenades: 140
Helmets: 137, 139, 140
Light machine pistols: 136
Machine guns: 138
Pistols: 139, 140
Uniforms: 39-41, 136, 138, 140
Water bottles: 137, 139, 140

JAPAN

Ammunition: 67, 146, 149
Bayonets: 67, 146
Caps: 141, 145, 148
Carbines: 66, 145, 148
Field rifles: 66, 145, 148
Gas masks: 143, 146, 149
Grenades: 67, 143, 146, 149
Helmets: 143, 145, 148
Machine guns: 142, 144, 147
Mortars: 147
Pistols: 66, 141, 143
Small field guns: 188
Sword: 141
Tanks: 185
Trenching tools: 143, 149
Uniforms: 9, 14, 42, 43, 141, 142, 144, 147
Water bottles: 67, 141, 143, 146, 149

POLAND

Ammunition: 153
Bayonets: 153
Caps: 150
Carbines: 150, 153, 171, 178
Field rifles: 152, 171
Grenades: 151
Helmets: 153
Light machine pistols: 150
Machine guns: 152
Pistols: 94, 151, 153
Revolver: 151
Trenching tools: 151
Uniforms: 44, 45, 150, 152

RUMANIA

Ammunition: 154
Bayonets: 153, 154
Caps: 154
Field guns: 154
Helmets: 154
Uniforms: 46, 154
Water bottles: 154

USA

Ammunition: 64, 75, 157, 161, 163, 165, 169
Antitank guns: 164
Bayonets: 64, 75, 157, 161
Caps: 157, 160, 163, 165, 169
Carbines: 74, 156, 160, 163, 168
Field rifles: 63, 156, 159, 160, 165, 167, 168
Grenades: 64, 75, 157, 161, 165, 168
Helmets: 64, 75, 157, 160, 163, 165, 169
Light machine pistols: 62, 73, 117, 120, 155, 162, 165, 167
Machine guns: 62, 73, 155, 158, 159, 162, 165, 166
Mortars: 186
Pistols: 63, 66, 74, 156, 160, 163, 168
Revolvers: 66, 168
Tanks: 184
Trenching tools: 143, 149, 157, 161, 169
Uniforms: 47-51, 155, 158, 162, 164, 166
Water bottles: 64, 75, 157, 161, 163, 169

USSR

Ammunition: 172, 175, 177, 179, 181
Bayonets: 172, 175, 177, 179
Caps: 181
Carbines: 171, 174, 176, 178, 181
Field rifles: 171, 174, 178
Gas masks: 172, 175, 177, 179
Grenades: 67, 151, 172, 175, 177, 180
Hats: 174, 177, 180
Helmets: 172, 174, 179
Light machine pistols: 65, 150, 170, 173, 178, 180
Machine guns: 170
Mortars: 187
Pistols: 151, 171
Revolvers: 151, 171
Small field guns: 189
Trenching tools: 151, 172, 175, 177, 180
Uniforms: 27, 30, 52-55, 170, 173, 176, 178, 180, 181
Water bottles: 172, 174, 177, 179, 180

YUGOSLAVIA

Ammunition: 182
Caps: 182
Field rifles: 182
Light machine pistols: 182
Uniforms: 56, 182
Water bottles: 182